WIND
IN THE
WILDERNESS

WIND
IN THE
WILDERNESS

A Lenten Study From the Prophets

DJ del Rosario

Abingdon Press / Nashville

ISBN-13: 9781501824319

16 17 18 19 20 21 22 23 24 25—10 9 8 7 6 5 4 3 2 1

Manufactured in the United States of America

Contents

Introduction

Thank you for taking the time to read this book; meeting you here is truly an honor. My hope for you is that you take the season of Lent as an opportunity to slow down, reflect, and authentically engage with God, who is active in our world today. Lent is a time of self-examination and penitence, and it is often demonstrated by self-denial in preparation for Easter, the time for celebrating resurrection and new life. Self-examination and penitence lead to renewal.

Early church father Irenaeus wrote about differences between the practices of Lenten fasting in the East and West. In AD 325, the Council of Nicaea established a forty-day Lenten season of fasting. The original intent of the forty-day Lenten fast may have been to prepare for baptism.[1] What we know is that the season of Lent eventually became important to the whole church. Lent is a time to prepare our physical and spiritual selves to remember Christ's victorious rising from the dead for humanity.

In both the East and the West, the observance of Lent was strict and serious. Pope Gregory wrote, "We abstain from flesh, meat, and from all things that come from flesh, as milk, cheese, and eggs." The rule was for one meal a day, at 3 p.m. or in the evening.[2] In 601, Pope Gregory moved the beginning of Lent to Wednesday, now called Ash Wednesday, forty-six days before Easter. He did this to secure the exact number of forty days in Lent—not counting Sundays, which were feast days. Gregory is also credited with the ceremony that gives the day Ash Wednesday its name. As Christians came to the church for forgiveness, Gregory marked their foreheads with ashes in the shape of a cross.[3] Biblically, the ashes symbolize repentance, grief, and the reality of mortality. They remind us of our frail humanity, captured in the words, "You are dust, and to dust you shall return" (Genesis 3:19 NRSV). Putting ashes on the forehead is like saying, "Welcome to the Lenten season. It's now time to remember that the human body will not last forever."

I believe that the Lenten season provides an opportunity for education and spiritual revival. It is a time for reflection and preparation. As we move through this season of Lent, we also have a chance to look deeply into the history of Jesus' life and to consider how Jesus, the Messiah, fulfilled the promises of the Hebrew prophets.

The title of this book is WIND IN THE WILDERNESS. Though we cannot see the wind, we know it by its effects and interpret it by its results. We see how wind can bend and move things. When something is affected by wind, we begin to take notice of its potential and power. The same can be said for the work of the Hebrew prophets, who communicated God's justice and faithfulness at various times throughout the history of God's people. Much of this history was chaotic and unpredictable, like the wilderness. Often times it felt as if God was distant. Yet as the prophets spoke, the wind of God's presence was blowing. Through their words the wind was moving, giving us a hint of Jesus, who was to come.

This Lenten study will focus on the Hebrew prophets and their message of justice. It will call readers to turn their attention to the issues of justice in today's world. Each chapter will explore a different prophet, highlighting how they challenged the Israelite people—and us—through God's word to live out God's justice. Each chapter will demonstrate how the prophetic message was fulfilled in the life and ministry of Jesus, preparing the way for his teaching, healing, death, and resurrection. The study will demonstrate continuity between the prophetic emphasis on justice and Jesus' proclamation of the kingdom of God. In the first four chapters, we will study the prophets, Isaiah, Jeremiah, Hosea, and Jonah, to understand how they portrayed God's vision of justice in their times and places, which often felt like the wilderness. In the fifth chapter, we will study the Book of Job. Though he wasn't a prophet, his book gives us powerful insights about how to be present in the waiting as we wait for God's justice to be fully revealed. In the sixth chapter, we will study Zechariah and discuss how his message helps us understand Jesus' entry into Jerusalem. The final chapter, corresponding to Easter Sunday, speaks of the resurrection of Jesus and how it brings God's justice to fulfillment. Through the pages of this book, I hope that you will see how the wind moved among God's people in the past, to discover how it's moving in your life today.

Special Thanks:

Thank you to the United Methodist Publishing House for taking a chance on a local pastor in Bothell, Washington. This book was inspired by a sermon series I preached in the 2016 Lenten Season. I'm so grateful for the people of Bothell United Methodist Church and the surrounding communities. God is doing something amazing and powerful in our growing community. Thanks to your faithfulness, your engagement, and deepening discipleship, this is more than a book. I'd like to thank Celeste Deveney and Reverend Joseph Kim for inspiration for the title of the book and its direction. A very special thanks to Candace Larson, who worked tirelessly as the initial copy editor of this book.

To my wife, Elaine, thank you for always encouraging me to work toward excellence. Thank you for putting up with my endless hours and all those deep theological talks that continue to shape my life and theology. For my three daughters, Sage, Hazel, and Scarlett: I serve as a pastor because I believe that the world doesn't have to be the way it currently is. My prayer is that this book may make one small step toward the world God intended it to be, full of grace and mercy for one and all. I dream of a time when all may have enough, where love wins, and none may question whether God loves them.

1. From *www.catholiceducation.org/en/culture/catholic-contributions/history-of-lent.html*. Accessed 21 September 2016.

2. From *www.catholiceducation.org/en/culture/catholic-contributions/history-of-lent.html*. Accessed 21 September 2016.

3. From *www.bibleinfo.com/en/questions/ash-wednesday-bible*. Accessed 21 September 2016.

Building a Skyscraper: Isaiah

Scripture: Read Isaiah 9:6-7; 53:1-6

A child is born to us, a son is given to us, and authority will be on his shoulders. He will be named Wonderful Counselor, Mighty God, Eternal Father, Prince of Peace. (Isaiah 9:6)

I first used a hammer and nails when I was a kid. I had no idea how to swing a hammer, but after watching *The Karate Kid*, I figured that I could put the nail in the wall in one swing. Since you may not know me, I'm going to play a little Captain Obvious: I was not the Karate Kid.

The first time I picked up a hammer was when my little United Methodist church was building a bigger sanctuary. We hired contractors to oversee the technical portion of the construction, but anything we could do on our own, we did. Looking back, I remember placing the first nail to the wall and knowing that I was a part of something bigger than myself. I had no idea what the sanctuary would eventually look like, but I knew this nail meant something so much greater than a single nail.

Not all construction projects are pleasant when you're in the middle of them. I once heard a friend talk about a long period of struggle she experienced when the company that employed her was going through a difficult time. At the start of the year, upper management set lofty corporate goals, and extra work was required in order to achieve those goals. After a long year of working extra hours, often late into the night, on endless projects, her year-end review consisted of criticism for her effort. She received none of the bonuses previously promised by upper management. Despite her team's best efforts, the company lost money. All that extra work led to a deep sense of loss.

A Big Hole

As my friend shared her story, she likened the work she'd done to building a skyscraper. In order to build a building that is worthy of the name of "skyscraper," you must first make a large hole. Years of preparation are required before one inch can be built upward.

Even the hole can't take shape right away. Imagine the necessary steps needed before a shovel can even break ground. Just to name a few of the steps, experts are needed to create blueprints; geologists are needed to study the landscape; and many conversations must occur between contractors and builders. Then, after all the pre-work is done, after all the necessary paperwork is signed, the digging finally begins. Imagine all the dirt that needs to be unearthed! And all that dirt must be moved somewhere, which can be very time consuming and expensive.

And the hole itself is just the start. Once the hole is dug, pipes need to be placed, a foundation must by poured, and time is required for everything to settle. All that work takes so much time. And what is your reward after building a foundation? One great big, expensive hole! That's what my friend told me that she felt after a long year of work. Months of hard work and you find yourself in one gigantic hole!

This season of Lent, we have a chance to pause and take a look around to see what kind of hole we are in, because let's face it, we are all in a hole of some kind or another. A great big hole isn't the finished product, but finding ourselves in holes can give us a chance to gain greater perspective on life and on what is happening around us.

Let's take a look at Isaiah 53. I wonder if the Israelites felt like they were sitting in the depths of a cavernous hole as they heard these words. The Book of Isaiah covers over two hundred years. Considering this incredible amount of time, many scholars believe that more than one prophet contributed to this book over this time period. Scholars often speak of "First Isaiah" as the author of most of Chapters 1–39, and "Second Isaiah" and "Third Isaiah" as the authors of Chapters 40–66. In Chapter 53, we hear the prophetic words of the anonymous prophet frequently referred to as Second Isaiah. The work of this prophet is found in Chapters 34–35 and 40–55. Biblical scholar Paul Hanson notes that this prophet is also known as Deutero-Isaiah, the Prophet of the Exile, or the Prophet of Consolation.[1]

These many titles suggest the sacred connection of the prophet Second Isaiah to the Israelite experience of exile, suffering, and their ultimate redemption. We don't know any details about the life of this prophet, but his specific life circumstances aren't critical. Our focus is on the prophet's calling for a time of justice and peace.

The words and actions of prophets were rooted distinctly in their time; they addressed political tensions as well as their cultural contexts. The prophet who wrote Isaiah 53 is no exception in his call for justice and peace. Second Isaiah's words were written about a half-century after a cultural catastrophe that left God's people broken, landless, and largely hopeless. In 587 BC, the Babylonian empire, led by King Nebuchadnezzar, attacked the kingdom of Judah, laid siege to Jerusalem, and eventually destroyed the city. The Babylonians deported many of the people of Judah and Jerusalem to exile in Babylon. For nearly fifty years, the people stayed in Babylon, far away from their ancestral land, with their holy city and its Temple lying in ruins. Into these circumstances, Second Isaiah communicated words of hope and comfort, lifting up a vision for a better future characterized by justice and peace. Isaiah 53 is part of this vision.

Much of the material written by Second Isaiah echoes the experience of the Exodus (see especially Isaiah 40), when God delivered the people from enslavement in Egypt many generations before. In Genesis 37-50, we read about Joseph, who was sold into slavery by his brothers (Genesis 37). In Genesis 46-47, after Joseph rises to power, he moves his father, brothers, and their clan to Egypt during a time of famine. In Egypt, the Israelites flourish through the end of Genesis. By the first chapter in Exodus, Joseph has died (at the ripe old age of 110), and his people are thriving. After the death of Joseph, a new Pharaoh comes to power who perceives the Israelites as a threat, ushering in the infamous enslavement of the Israelite people in the Book of Exodus. But God never wastes a crisis. God acted powerfully through Moses and miraculous events to bring the people out of slavery in Egypt, lead them through the wilderness, and establish them in their own land, the land that became the kingdoms of Israel and Judah. By drawing a deliberate connection between the Babylonian exile after 587 BC and the slavery in Egypt many centuries before, Second Isaiah gave a word of hope to the people. Just as God brought them out of Egypt and established them in the land, God would now bring them out of Babylon and establish them anew.

Building a Skyscraper

The prophet Isaiah's words in Chapters 9 and 53 harken back to visions of what God will do and what was yet to come when all seemed lost. These verses would resonate with the Israelite people during their time of exile in Babylon because the words promised that God would redeem them.

Let's look first at Isaiah 9:1-7.

[1] Nonetheless, those who were in distress won't be exhausted. At an earlier time, God cursed the land of Zebulun

and the land of Naphtali, but later he glorified the way of the sea, the far side of the Jordan, and the Galilee of the nations.

> ² The people walking in darkness have seen a great light.
>> On those living in a pitch-dark land, light has dawned.
> ³ You have made the nation great;
>> you have increased its joy.
> They rejoiced before you as with joy at the harvest,
>> as those who divide plunder rejoice.
> ⁴ As on the day of Midian, you've shattered the yoke that burdened them,
>> the staff on their shoulders,
>> and the rod of their oppressor.
> ⁵ Because every boot of the thundering warriors,
>> and every garment rolled in blood
>> will be burned, fuel for the fire.
> ⁶ A child is born to us, a son is given to us,
>> and authority will be on his shoulders.
>> He will be named
>> Wonderful Counselor, Mighty God,
>> Eternal Father, Prince of Peace.
> ⁷ There will be vast authority and endless peace
>> for David's throne and for his kingdom,
>> establishing and sustaining it
>> with justice and righteousness
>> now and forever.

The zeal of the LORD of heavenly forces will do this.

Isaiah 9 was most likely a coronation hymn during the time of First Isaiah. But when we read it within the context of the whole book, we see that it resonates with the hope that Second Isaiah lifts up. The people have been "distressed" and "walking in darkness," but light and joy are about to break forth (Isaiah 9:1-3). The passage envisions a just king who will establish God's eternal peace: "There will be vast authority and endless peace for David's throne and for his kingdom, establishing and sustaining it with justice and righteousness now and forever" (Isaiah 9:7). Redemption is more than just being freed from enslavement. It includes the establishment of peace, justice, and righteousness, by none other than the "Prince of Peace" himself (Isaiah 9:6). This dramatic vision of the future is like the plan for a finished skyscraper, a blueprint of what life would be like when God's construction project is completed.

Now let's consider Isaiah 53:1-6.

¹ Who can believe what we have heard,
   and for whose sake has the LORD's arm been revealed?
² He grew up like a young plant before us,
   like a root from dry ground.
He possessed no splendid form for us to see,
   no desirable appearance.
³ He was despised and avoided by others;
   a man who suffered, who knew sickness well.
Like someone from whom people hid their faces,
   he was despised, and we didn't think about him.

⁴ It was certainly our sickness that he carried,
   and our sufferings that he bore,
   but we thought him afflicted,
   struck down by God and tormented.
⁵ He was pierced because of our rebellions
   and crushed because of our crimes.
   He bore the punishment that made us whole;
   by his wounds we are healed.
⁶ Like sheep we had all wandered away,
   each going its own way,
   but the LORD let fall on him all our crimes.

Isaiah 53:1-6 is in the fourth of four servant passages included in the work of Second Isaiah (Isaiah 52:13–53:12). These passages describe an anonymous servant, chosen by God to bring justice to the nations. The other servant passages are Isaiah 42:1-4, Isaiah 49:1-6, and Isaiah 50:4-9. We also find a reference to many nations in the fourth servant passage: "But he will astonish many nations. Kings will be silenced because of him, because they will see what they haven't seen before; what they haven't heard before, they will ponder" (Isaiah 52:15). God's plan for redemption isn't about one tribe, one people. It demands justice to and from every nation, every tribe, and everyone.

The time spent in exile was crucial to the identity formation of the people of Israel. During these times of exile, they reflected on what it meant to be the people of God. While they lived in exile as a conquered people, their spiritual, emotional, and even physical sufferings always pointed to the need to understand what it meant to be God's people. Can you guess how they might have felt in these circumstances? To return to my friend's story about a skyscraper, the people in exile must have felt as if they were in a huge hole, wondering if there was any way out of it. Passages like Isaiah 9 had painted a glorious vision; the skyscraper was prophesied to come. But their experience and their parents' experience had been one of pain, destruction, and little to show for their best efforts. Isaiah's word came when the people were still stuck looking up from the hole they found themselves in. How did the people of Israel arrive at such a state? How did they get themselves into such a hole? How did their actions or inactions play a role in their current situation? Who was this "servant" that Isaiah prophesied about? When would justice and peace finally come?

The final two servant songs, Isaiah 50:4-9 and 52:13–53:12, describe a servant who suffers. This servant "gave [his] body to attackers" and "didn't hide [his] face from insults and spitting" (Isaiah 50:6). He was "despised and avoided," well-acquainted with suffering, "like someone from whom people hid their faces" (Isaiah 52:3). The suffering servant has done no wrong. Unlike the exiled people, the servant has not turned to other gods, fallen into the trap of politics, or fallen into a pattern of behaviors that caused others harm.

The suffering servant doesn't beg for mercy for himself; he lives, suffers, and dies on behalf others.

Christians look to these passages to describe God's work in and through Jesus Christ. These words in Isaiah paint a picture of scandalous love by showing how Jesus dies on behalf of the very worst in us, in humankind. It's one thing to say that Jesus loves you or that Jesus loves me. What does it mean to say that Jesus loves people who choose financial profit over just wages? What about folks who choose to do harm? Could Jesus' love possibly be available to people who commit acts of terror against other nations or in homes of the innocent? Where is the justice in that? How can the Messiah love people like them? God may love me in my khakis and approve of my clean-cut look, but could God love humanity, whose hands are stained with the blood of the innocent?

> He was despised and avoided by others;
> a man who suffered, who knew sickness well.
> Like someone from whom people hid their faces,
> he was despised, and we didn't think about him.
> It was certainly our sickness that he carried,
> and our sufferings that he bore. (Isaiah 53:3-4a)

Jesus the Messiah took on the worst of us, the very worst of what we are capable of, so that we might have a chance to be who we were created to be. He is the skyscraper that God is building, that God indeed has built. The hole—the suffering—wasn't the end for the people in exile. It isn't the end for us.

The Hole Isn't the Finished Product

Lent is a chance for us to become more intentional with our time. It can be so easy and tempting to move mindlessly from one day to the next. This season offers a beautiful opportunity to slow down and pay attention to the many ways the Holy Spirit is moving and engaging in our world.

The hole we are in isn't the end; the skyscraper, the kingdom is our goal. Let's not lose sight of why we are here.

The truth is that we are all in a hole. Lent is a time for us to evaluate our sacred rituals, our everyday spiritual practices, and choose to delve deeper. We can consider the incredible love that Jesus has by fasting, repenting, and practicing spiritual disciplines. Fasting is a time of intentionally not eating food for a set amount of time. For example, when the hunger pains might begin to occur, these physical needs and desires may offer a chance for us to remember Jesus' sacrifice or to be in solidarity with those who are less fortunate. We might abstain from alcohol or meat or sugars. Reverend Dottie Escobedo-Frank wrote a great study for Lent entitled *Give It UP!* that is full of practical modern spiritual disciplines that I recommend.[2] Purposely changing our rhythm during Lent can be like a great vacation; it provides a glimpse of how life could be less complicated and more attuned to creation and the Creator.

If you have observed Lent before, this season of reflection matters because, for the vast majority of us, we can all use a healthier pace of rhythm for our lives. It's also possible that this is the first time that you are choosing to engage in Lent. If this is your first time, I'm so glad that you have chosen this book as an opportunity to engage with both your head and your heart. My prayer is that this time of discernment will also inspire you to help make our world a better place. Sometimes the hole we're in gets too deep and we forget why we started digging in the first place. We need this season to remember that the hole isn't the finished product; it's the beginning of the foundation.

The Lenten season begins with the reminder that we will all die one day, but death is not the final product. This life isn't the final product either. I believe that the world we live in today doesn't have to be the way it is. Racism, homophobia, xenophobia, classism, sexism, and all the things that drive wedges between us are meant to pass.

I serve at Bothell United Methodist Church. Bothell United Methodist Church was the first church in the city of Bothell,

Washington, and has been around for more than 130 years. The people are amazing, the city is gorgeous, and the sanctuary will take your breath away pretty much any time of day. During the church's construction, a solitary beam was laid aside for a special purpose. Church members had the opportunity to write their name on the beam before it was placed, making their mark on the future. When the people of the church were building their new sanctuary, many imagined that beam would be there for many generations to come. But before the beam was placed, before the final touches were completed in this sacred space, we needed a hole in order to lay a proper foundation.

Sometimes we feel like we are in a great big pit. Let's not forget, the hole isn't the final product. No matter how big our pit may feel, we worship Jesus who reminds us that our world isn't finished yet. This hole isn't the end. Jesus invites us right here and now to see that there is so much more to building this skyscraper than a hole. If we read just a little farther, we will find that Isaiah 58:9-10, which was written after the people returned from Exile in Babylon, describes what the skyscraper may look like:

> Then you will call, and the Lord will answer;
> you will cry for help, and God will say, "I'm here."
> If you remove the yoke from among you,
> the finger-pointing, the wicked speech;
> if you open your heart to the hungry,
> and provide abundantly for those who are afflicted,
> your light will shine in the darkness,
> and your gloom will be like the noon.

Questions for Reflection and Discussion

1. When have you felt like you worked really hard and ended up in a big hole you didn't anticipate?
2. How did you respond?
3. How did the experience challenge you?

4. Where have you experienced the peace and hope of Jesus?
5. What holes do you see in your community or in society around you?
6. What would you name as your skyscraper in this season?
7. How can holding on to a vision of the finished product— God's justice—help you find courage and strength in the hole?

Prayer

Loving and gracious God, thank you so much for the season of Lent. Thank you for this opportunity to slow down, reflect, and ponder what kind of holes we find ourselves in. Thank you that these holes are never meant to be a finished product, rather they are a sign of work in progress. By your grace, we are so grateful for the weeks ahead of us where we can ponder your amazing love. We know that the kingdom is coming. May this season be more than an opportunity for spouting lofty words; may it also be a chance to deepen our discipleship. This we pray in your Son's name, Jesus the Christ. Amen.

Focus for the Week

Take 5 minutes each day to ask yourself: What might be holding me back in this season of Lent to fully being present? Allow yourself the time to write your responses and by the end of the week, offer your responses as a prayer to God.

Read the following Scriptures each day. Pause prayerfully before you read. Become aware of your breathing, of the ways you are drawn to this sacred moment, and of the ways you may be distracted. Offer all that is happening to God. Ask for God's guidance as you engage each of the readings.

Monday: Luke 3:23-31 *thru*
Tuesday: John 13:3 *fri*
Wednesday: 1 Timothy 3:16 *sat*
Thursday: Jeremiah 23:1-4 *sun*
Friday: Jeremiah 23:5-8 *mon*
Saturday: Jeremiah 23:1-8 *tues.*

1. From *Isaiah 40-66: Interpretation: A Bible Commentary for Teaching and Preaching*, by Paul D. Hanson (Westminster John Knox Press); page 2.

2. *Give It Up! A Lenten Study for Adults*, by Dottie Escobedo-Frank (Abingdon Press, 2014).

Sticks and Stones: Jeremiah

Scripture: Read Jeremiah 23:1-8

The time is coming, declares the LORD, when I will raise up a righteous descendant from David's line, and he will rule as a wise king. He will do what is just and right in the land. . . . And his name will be The LORD Is Our Righteousness.

(Jeremiah 23:5-6)

Will you help me finish the following statement? "Sticks and Stones may break my bones, but words ___ ____ ____ me."

In Chapter 1, I compared the kingdom of God to a skyscraper to explore the words of the prophet Isaiah. In this chapter, we will dive into the prophet Jeremiah's words in Jeremiah 23. In preparation of this chapter, I asked my congregation and contacts on social media to share something that they heard during the course of their lives that was formative to them. Here are just a few examples of the responses that I received:

- Never pass up a lemonade stand. It's the motto of my family of origin. The literal interpretation is held with strict rigidity. But the idea at the crux of it translates to a lot more of life's opportunities.

- We carry high expectations for each other and low expectations for God when we should carry low expectations for each other and high expectations for God.
- Most people do the best they are able to do. This has helped me to stop judging harshly.
- My dad said, "What you permit, you promote. I've used this at home and at work."
- My mom told me, "I don't think you are capable of love."

Most of these are positive, but that last one is strikingly negative. Based on this, would you agree that words can hurt? I believe they can. I still carry the scars and memories of words people said to me years ago. Sticks and stones can do real damage. So can words. But as the first examples above show, words can also heal. The words of people we trust, people who influence our lives, can impact us significantly, for good or for bad. What about words from God?

Bad Shepherds

Words from God can make a difference, especially when the timing is right. The first twenty-eight chapters of Jeremiah focus on the judgment of the Hebrew people. Jeremiah 10:21 provides a great glimpse of the prophet's feelings toward the religious and political leaders in that time: "The shepherd kings have lost their senses." In the Bible, leaders are often described as shepherds, those who lead and care for the people, the sheep. But the leaders in Jeremiah's time were preying on their own people. We see this described in strong language in Jeremiah 23, where the shepherds "destroy and scatter the sheep of my pasture" (23:1). In the words of biblical commentator John Guest, they have been "fleecing the flock." Author Philip Ryken has said, "It is hard for sheep to trust a shepherd who eats mutton chops for dinner, is it not? With shepherds like these, who needs wolves?" [2]

Which leaders did Jeremiah have in mind, and what had they done to fail the people? The little nation of Judah was having a hard time in Jeremiah's day; the once great Assyrian empire was waning and a new empire, Babylon, was picking up momentum. By the 600s BC, the Babylonians finished off what was left of the Assyrian Empire and moved toward Egypt. The newly minted leader of the Hebrew people, Jehoiakim, had a tough decision to make. David Garber Jr., associate professor of Old Testament and Hebrew at McAfee School of Theology in Atlanta, Georgia, provides a great snapshot of the political landscape in Jeremiah's time:

> One of Judah's shepherds, Jehoiakim, chose poorly and withheld tribute from Babylon, angering the Babylonians who invaded Jerusalem shortly after Jehoiakim's death. The Babylonians took his successor, Jehoiachin, into exile with the upper class leaders of Jerusalem, and replaced him with Zedekiah. Zedekiah, however, was another bad shepherd, who by 590 BCE, decided to withhold tribute once again to Babylon, against the advisement of Jeremiah (see Jeremiah 27:4-8).[3]

The "shepherds" the prophet was referring to in Jeremiah 23 were people like Jehoiakim and Zedekiah. The Babylonians were demanding tributes (or taxes) from Judah. But these leaders chose not to pay the Babylonian bullies and instead put their people in danger. Their failed leadership cost the people their freedom and sent them into exile. They scattered and destroyed the "sheep of [God's] pasture" (Jeremiah 23:1). Shepherds are supposed to protect their flock, care for them, defend against attackers, and find them when they are lost. In Jeremiah's time, the leaders of Judah abused their power over and over again. They were trusted with the power and given the authority to care for the people. But the shepherds hurt their sheep.

Shepherds aren't supposed to hurt their sheep. Not by their actions and certainly not by their inactions. The responsibility of the shepherd is to lay his life down for the sheep if necessary. Jesus told a parable about a shepherd who left ninety-nine sheep to search for one that was lost (see Luke 15:3-7 and Matthew 18:10-14), demonstrating God's love for each individual person. I recognize this love from personal experience. In seminary, my instructor warned the class against using personal stories to illustrate the love of Jesus. Theologically, it would be irresponsible of me to make you believe that my love for my daughters can directly compare to the love Jesus has for each of us. While I love my girls with all that I am, comparing my love to Jesus' love for us simply isn't a fair comparison. The deep and absolute love I have for my daughters does not compare to the sacrifice and care Jesus has for every person. That said, I'd like to share an example that might help us begin to understand what Jesus might have meant when he told the parable about lost sheep.

My favorite day of the week is Friday. On Fridays, I get to take my three girls out to play. Father-daughters time is sacred time to me. We go many places like parks, museums, the zoo, or the mountains. Without fail, wherever we go, I find myself looking around to locate all the exits, all the people, and assessing the safety so my kids can play. Being outnumbered three to one, I occasionally lose track of one of my girls and I have to search for them. After checking the obvious spots, I find myself looking for the lost child in places that I hope that she is not—places out of my direct line-of-sight, like bathrooms. The moment I find her, I can relate to the sense of joy that the shepherd of Jesus' parable felt when he found the one lost sheep and returned to the ninety-nine others. Imagine if I came home to my spouse and said, "Look honey, I brought home two out of three of our girls! Pretty good odds." If I came home with that attitude, I would have some explaining to do. In much the same way, every sheep counts to the shepherd. It's not just the shepherd's job; his life's mission is to protect the sheep.

When prophet Jeremiah referred to the leaders as shepherds and described their harmful and negligent actions, this imagery was meant to be an outright insult. And everyone in his time would have known it. Everyone would have known it because most everyone in that time understood the primary roles and responsibilities of shepherds. Jeremiah says that their leaders have scattered the flock and driven them away (23:2). Instead of guarding the sheep, the shepherds have destroyed them.

The Lord Is Our Righteousness

One of the key shepherds who abused his power was a leader named Zedekiah. Zedekiah was the last king of Judah before the destruction of the kingdom by the Babylonian empire. Old Testament professor David G. Garber Jr. does a wonderful job unpacking the leaders in Jeremiah's time and the significance of Jeremiah's words about them. As Garber points out, Zedekiah's name means "the Lord is my righteousness." Fast forward to Jeremiah 23:5-6, where the prophet speaks of the coming righteous and wise king whose name will be "The Lord Is Our Righteousness." The similarity to Zedekiah, "the Lord is my righteousness," is unmistakable. Jeremiah deliberately contrasts the coming righteous leader with the present leader, Zedekiah, the shepherd who has failed the sheep.[4]

Jeremiah prophesies on behalf of God, "The time is coming, declares the LORD, when I will raise up a righteous descendant from David's line, and he will rule as a wise king. He will do what is just and right in the land. During his lifetime, Judah will be saved and Israel will live in safety. And his name will be The LORD Is Our Righteousness" (verses 5-6).

Sticks and stones. Words can hurt and words can heal. Jeremiah offers God's extraordinary promise of healing in words like *righteous, just, right,* and *righteousness.* These words are closely related in the original language and carry circles of meaning that embrace God's character as well the characters of individuals and communities. It is difficult to separate justice and righteousness. The words are healing

righteousness - in right relationship

27

words. When Jeremiah names the righteous king "The LORD Is Our Righteousness," he names the character of God and of the community.

I love how Garber points out this change from the first person singular to the plural. Instead of being all about me, what I need, how I can be righteous, "The Lord Is Our Righteousness" makes it about the whole people of Judah together. Being, living, acting right before God is meant to be done in community. So, while the leaders of the Judah looked out for themselves and ultimately put the people in danger, the ironic shift from the name of Zedekiah to the name of the righteous king who would come reminds the people of Judah of the importance of community. The leaders and the community are called to be just and righteous just as God is just and righteous.

Jeremiah might choose a different analogy than shepherds if he were prophesying to us today. Perhaps doctors and patients are easier for us to relate to than shepherds and sheep. A doctor's primary concern is caring for his or her patient. Can you imagine not being able to trust your own doctor? Maybe you don't trust doctors right now. What makes you not trust doctors? Imagine that you do have a doctor that you trust. What if every time you got medical advice, you had to wonder if you should question your doctor's motivation or wonder if he or she had a secret agenda? What if all doctors were notoriously known for serving themselves only? If that were true, how would you feel the next time you had to visit your doctor? Judah's leaders were supposed to be caring for the people, and instead they were abusing their authority.

Abuse by those in authority. That happened then and sadly it happens even today. Can you think of a few examples of people in authority who abuse their position? What about elected officials who spout hate, xenophobia, or lies in order to gain advantage? That's the world the people in Jeremiah's day were living in. In many ways, we are still living in that world today.

But, that's just the first two verses in Jeremiah 23. To stop after these verses is like reading "Sleeping Beauty" and closing the book after the princess pricks her finger on the spinning wheel and falls asleep. There is so much more to the story! As we have already seen, the Lord promised to set things right. Justice is coming! "I myself will gather," God says—God will act personally to care for the sheep and raise up good shepherds who will care for them (23:3-4). It's time for a change in leadership, but Jeremiah tells us that newness and hope are coming. The people and leaders have failed, but as theologian Walter Bruggemann puts it, "God's hope overrides that historical, covenantal failure."[6] I like the way the New Revised Standard Version translates verse 5: "The days are surely coming, says the Lord, when I will raise up for David a righteous Branch, and he shall reign as king and deal wisely, and shall execute justice and righteousness in the land." David, a shepherd, is famous in Scripture for defeating the Philistine bully Goliath with a sling (1 Samuel 17). He ultimately is anointed king and unites Israel and Judah. David is also an ancestor of Jesus the Messiah (Matthew 1:1-17; Luke 3:23-38). In this verse, Jeremiah brings a reminder of the past and hope for the future together. It is in David's descendant, the Messiah, that Jeremiah's words are fulfilled.

Recently, a group of leaders from Bothell United Methodist Church went to a training event for Seattle laity in Des Moines, Washington. During a small-group reflection time, we got to talk about why we go to church. A person in my small group said to me, "You can't say you have to go to church because it's your job. Why do you, DJ, go to church?" I responded, "I go to church because church reminds me every week that God can even love me, but God doesn't just love me. The liturgical seasons, like Lent, are beautiful reminders that church is meant to be a time of slowing down enough to notice where God is already working, to experience how God is working through others, and to remember that we are all in this together."

Zedekiah means "the LORD is *my* righteousness". He was one bad shepherd who didn't consider his flock. Jeremiah was moved to deep irony in the promise of restoration in

They thought they buried us, not knowing we are seeds

29

Jeremiah 23:1-8. In that promise, Zedekiah's name moved from "me" to "we." The contrast between his name and the name of the promised righteous descendant from David's line tells much of the story. His name would be "The LORD Is *Our* Righteousness." That seems about right. Jeremiah's irony underscores the difference between the kings of his day and the promised righteous king. Sticks and stones. Words can impact our lives in powerful ways.

Jeremiah's promise of a righteous and just king in verses 5-6 speak profoundly to Christians about Jesus Christ. While I was writing this chapter, famous author Harper Lee died. She was the author *To Kill a Mockingbird*. One of my favorite quotes from her book is, "You never really understand a person until you consider things from his point of view . . . until you climb into his skin and walk around in it."[6] Jesus walked around in our skin. He chose to be born in this world, feel sickness, taste loneliness, and know what it means to be in our skin. That's the God we worship: God who chooses us time and time again. The one who created us and who loves us deeply. God, revealed in Jesus, whose actions and words exemplified justice and righteousness. Words don't just impact *me*. Words have the power to impact the *we*. How will your words shape your communities this week?

Questions for Reflection and Discussion

1. What does the saying, "Sticks and stones will break my bones, but words will never hurt me" mean to you?
2. When do your words speak louder than actions?
3. Where and how do you hear God calling you to listen, act, and respond today?
4. How will your words shape your communities this week?
5. What is the difference between "my righteousness" and "our righteousness"? How can we pursue righteousness together rather than seeking it only for ourselves?

6. Where do you see community leaders looking out for themselves only? What about religious leaders? What might the prophet Jeremiah say to such leaders today?
7. What hope do you see for the church in Jeremiah's words about a righteous and wise king? How can Jesus' presence in the world fulfill this hope?

Prayer

Loving and gracious God, far too often we spend time as humanity hurting one another with our actions, inactions, and words. Forgive us for the times when we step aside when you ask us to step up. Help us in the moments when we can speak up for those who are hurting and in need. Teach us to be people who acknowledge our hurts and pains as well as the struggles in others. Open our eyes to see more than what is before us. Help us to see opportunities to be your living grace and peace here and now. Thanks be to you, loving God. Amen.

Focus for the Week

Take time this week to talk with someone you trust about words that have hurt you in the past; take time to talk about how to take one step closer from hurt to healing. Spend time each day looking for opportunities to provide support and comfort to people in the places where you live, work, play, and learn. Stretch yourself beyond engaging in a good deed and look for a chance to exemplify Jesus' love.

Read the following Scriptures each day. Pause prayerfully before you read. Become aware of your breathing, of the ways you are drawn to this sacred moment, and of the ways you may be distracted. Offer all that is happening to God. Ask for God's guidance as you engage each of the readings.

Monday: Hosea 1:1-9
Tuesday: Hosea 1:2-4
Wednesday: Hosea 1:5-6
Thursday: Hosea 1:7-9
Friday: Hosea 11:1-4
Saturday: Hosea 1:1-9

1. From *Jeremiah, Lamentations: The Communicator's Commentary*, by John Guest (Word, 1988); page 170.

2. From *Jeremiah and Lamentations: From Sorrow to Hope*, by Philip G. Ryken (Redesign edition, Crossway, 2012); page 336.

3. From *www.workingpreacher.org/preaching.aspx?commentary_id=1391#post_comments.* Accessed 22 September 2016.

4. From *www.workingpreacher.org/preaching.aspx?commentary_id=1391#post_comments.* Accessed 22 September 2016.

5. From *A Commentary on Jeremiah: Exile and Homecoming*, by Walter Bruggemann (Eerdmans, 1998); page 206.

6. From *To Kill a Mockingbird*, by Harper Lee (Mass Market Paperback; Grand Central Publishing, 1988); page 39.

Worst Baby Names EVER: Hosea

Scripture: Read Hosea 1:1-9 and Hosea 11:1-4

When Israel was a child, I loved him, . . .
I led them
>*with bands of human kindness,*
>*with cords of love.*
>*I treated them like those*
>>*who lift infants to their cheeks;*
>>*I bent down to them and fed them. (Hosea 11:1, 4)*

I love technology. There, I said it. I've loved technology since I remember using a rotary phone and watching in awe as the dial spun back every time I picked a number. I suppose my love of such things was natural; my father worked for a phone company. When I started driving, my parents let me borrow their Motorola flip phone. I think I had something like 16 minutes a month. Technology can be beautiful. Now, I preach using an iPad for my notes. I write sermons on my laptop. I love using social media platforms like Facebook and Instagram. There is something beautiful about the warm glow of the screen that makes me happy. Technology enhances my life.

I once went to a concert of one of my favorite artists and used social media to perfect my experience. While the musicians were warming up a message appeared on the jumbo screen, inviting us to post a picture and song request to Instagram using the event hashtag (#selfie). It's now common to engage through social media in real time with virtual strangers who are experiencing the same event by using the event hashtag. #Hashtags are used to simplify the search process for social media users by stringing peoples' comments, interactions, and collective thoughts together under one topic.

Sure enough, within seconds hundreds of us were using Instagram to post our selfies with the song we wanted the band, our band, to play. You can be sure that I engaged wholeheartedly. Here was my train of thought:

Post as many unique selfies as I could. My goal was to get as many favorite songs as possible played that night.

Post and repost my pictures across every media platform possible: Twitter, Facebook, Pinterest; if you can name it, I used it!

While I was posting online, the jumbo screen displayed a gigantic digital clock counting down the minutes and seconds to the time the concert would start. With the countdown, the screen flashed pictures of people who had posted online using the event hashtag. By the time the band finished warming up, the biggest screen I have ever seen began counting down the top ten songs that would be played—one at a time. My heart was racing faster with each song displayed. By the time the top three songs were displayed, only one of the songs I had requested was picked and I held my breath hoping, waiting, and willing for more of my favorite songs to be displayed. And then, they appeared on the screen. I got them! I screamed and clapped so wildly; I grabbed my cell phone and took a fifteen-second clip of the crowd cheering with me. Almost everyone was on their phone taking pictures, posting online, or waving their illuminated cell phones frantically. All of this happened before the band played a single note. Whew!

I often wonder how the prophets of the Hebrew Scriptures might have fared if given the tools we have today. In this age of information, we can find sermons that are centuries old, access countless theological treatises, and communicate and connect through social media in ways our world has never seen before. The concert experience described above is just one example. Might the prophets have used social media to amplify their message, or to shape their thought processes through meaningful conversations?

Strange Instructions, Unfortunate Names

The early prophets didn't have the same luxuries we do today. They couldn't Tweet, Snapchat, or use Facebook or Instagram to compare their experiences to others. They couldn't immediately share those moments the Lord spoke into their lives and took hold of them. Instead, when prophets heard God's voice, they had to discern it independently and decide for themselves the validity of what they were hearing. And they had to find creative, sometimes drastic ways to make their message known.

The Book of Hosea opens with the metaphor of the prophet's family as a sign of God's relationship to Israel. Almost right away, we see that it was a strained relationship. "The LORD said to him, 'Go, marry a prostitute and have children of prostitution, for the people of the land commit great prostitution by deserting the LORD'" (Hosea 1:2). In response, Hosea married a woman named Gomer, who may have been a prostitute or been involved in fertility rituals associated with the worship of Baal. In any case, the sense is that God has instructed Hosea to marry a sexually promiscuous woman, and he has done so in marrying Gomer. The marriage symbolizes God's relationship with Israel, where Gomer is a symbol of Israel as God's unfaithful spouse.

Can you imagine what might have been going through Hosea's mind as he received these instructions from God? This is the kind of lesson that no one would want to take part in! Then came the baby names. God commanded that Hosea and Gomer have children and specified what their names should be: Jezreel (recalling a history that will lead to punishment for the house of Jehu and Israel), No Compassion, and Not My People (Hosea 1:4-9).

What would Hosea have done if he'd had a chance to reach his peers through social media and ask them about what he was hearing from God? "Um, hey. Has God asked you to marry a prostitute just to teach Israel a lesson? Or is it just me?" I wonder what might have been going through his mind as he tried to decide what to do. How could he serve as a prophetic voice for God while publicly struggling in his own marriage? What would the people of Israel think? And why did he have to drag his children into the picture more deeply still, by giving them these bizarre and unfortunate names?

I have a friend who named the family dog Karma. The family has a great sense of humor as they call their dog's name at the dog park, "Good Karma!" Or sometimes "Bad Karma, don't do that!" Naming your dog something clever is one thing, but doing so for one's own children is different. Would anyone trust Hosea's words if they looked at the brokenness of his family, symbolized in the names of his children?

I asked my congregation and social media friends to share some of their favorite names and a brief explanation for each of them. Here are a few of their responses:

- **Claudia** is the name of our first grandchild who was named after my sister who died nine months before she was born.
- **Adeline "Addie"** is the character from a book that I read as a child with my mother. The character was strong and survived through a very difficult time for both her race and gender. It had an impact on me.
- **Xavier** because I like X names.

That last response was from one of our younger persons and was one of my favorite responses.

These are some examples of names that folks love; now, let's consider the names of Hosea and Gomer's kids. The names are symbols that express God's judgment of Israel and the ruling dynasty of Jehu, of which King Jeroboam II is the latest member. The children's names symbolize God's disapproval of Israel's unfaithfulness in their worship of other deities and political alliances with other nations.

Hosea's and Gomer's first child, a son, was named *Jezreel* because the punishment of the house of Jehu and Israel was coming. Jezreel is a place name for the fertile valley in which the houses or dynasties of Ahab and Jehu shed much blood in battles. Jehu, Jeroboam II's ancestor, became the ruler of Israel after a bloody battle against Ahab's dynasty. It was in the city of Jezreel that Jehu killed Ahab and his wife, Jezebel (2 Kings 9-10). The name of Hosea's first child symbolizes that this blood guilt will not go unpunished, but God will avenge it.

Hosea's second child, a daughter, was named *Lo-Ruhamah* or *No Compassion* because God is *done* doling out compassion and forgiveness to Israel. Their third child, a son, was named *Lo-ammi* or *Not My People* because, as his name not so subtly suggests, God is disowning Israel. You can't make this stuff up. Read Hosea 1:4-9.

James Limburg, professor emeritus of Old Testament at Luther Seminary, notes that Hosea was likely an older teenager at the beginning of this book.[1] I think of Hosea as a junior in high school. Yahweh didn't specify which woman Hosea should marry; the only criterion was her career choice—prostitution—if indeed it was a choice. We have no idea how Hosea chose Gomer as the woman who would fulfill this command from God. Consider other famous couples in the Bible: Abram and Sarai, Zechariah and Elizabeth; most had trouble conceiving. This is not the case for Hosea and Gomer; they don't seem to have any problem having children. Hosea heard God's calling, got married, had three children, and gave them incredibly unfortunate names.

Divine Loyalty

Hosea's marriage and the birth of his children symbolize a sad reality: Time and time again the people of Israel would break their covenant with Yahweh. Which part of the covenant? The part in which they must worship and be loyal to God alone. The people turn away from the God who rescued and delivered them out of slavery in Egypt, choosing to worship pieces of wood (Hosea 4:12). Check out Hosea 4 to learn about the details of their many sins. The chapter begins with Israel's lack of faithful love toward God. "There's no faithful love or loyalty, and no knowledge of God in the land" (4:1). The Hebrew word translated "faithful love" is *hesed*. We'll get to the broad meaning of that word shortly, but "faithful love" expresses it closely. Part of the Israelites' covenant with God was to show this faithful love or loyalty to God alone. They were clearly in violation of the covenant that Yahweh made with them, worshiping other options as deities. The only thing more amazing than their infidelity to Yahweh is Yahweh's faithfulness to Israel.

Hosea's loyalty to Gomer, who engages in prostitution and adultery (Hosea 2:1), can be considered as a metaphor for what God experienced with Israel. In the end, the faithfulness of the Lord was not dependent on the actions of the people of Israel, just as Hosea's fidelity was not dependent upon his wife's choices.

Let's revisit Hosea's and Gomer's youngest child. *Not My People* has enormous theological and historical implications. In Exodus 6:7 and Leviticus 26:12, God calls the Israelite people "God's people." In both verses, God promises to "take you as my people, and I'll be your God" (Exodus 6:7). This commitment to be Israel's God, and to recognize them as God's people, is an expression of God's faithfulness. When God commands Hosea to name his child Not My People, it symbolizes how the people's actions have broken the covenant. "Name him Not My people," God said, "because you are not my people, and I am not your God" (Hosea 1:9).

And yet, faithfulness has the last word. Later in the same chapter, God promises a reversal, in which those who have been called not-my-people will be called "Children of the living God" (Hosea 1:10). Faithfulness is at the heart of Hosea's relationship with Gomer, just as faithfulness is at the heart of God's relationship with Israel. Dr. Katharine Doob-Sakenfeld names this faithfulness as *hesed* in her book *Faithfulness in Action*.

Hesed applies to both God and God's people. The word *hesed* doesn't directly translate to English because it is more complex than one word. It interweaves love, kindness, steadfastness, loyalty, and commitment. It's a way of relating, and in this case *hesed* is the act of intentional presence. A difference exists between simply being physically present and choosing to be mentally and emotionally aware and engaged. Intentional presence involves all these aspects. How powerful is it to consider that no matter how unfaithful Gomer was to Hosea, he chose to remain intentionally present and engaged with her? Hosea's relationship, as unconventional as it was, was a glimpse into the *hesed* of God.

In Hosea 11, we find the image of a parent and child used as a metaphor, recalling the journey through the wilderness after the Exodus. Once again, God's love and faithfulness to Israel is clear:

I led them
>with bands of human kindness,
>with cords of love.
I treated them like those
>who lift infants to their cheeks;
>I bent down to them and fed them.
>>(Hosea 11:4)

God's relationship with Israel began with God's faithfulness, as God called them out of Egypt, taught them to walk, and tenderly nurtured them as a mother does an infant

(Hosea 11:1-4). It was the people who went astray, "sacrificing to the Baals" and "burning incense to idols" (11:2). "My people are bent on turning away from me," God says (11:7). And yet, God's faithfulness again has the last word:

How can I give you up, Ephraim?
　　How can I hand you over, Israel?
　How can I make you like Admah?
　　How can I treat you like Zeboiim?
My heart winces within me;
　　my compassion grows warm and tender.

I won't act on the heat of my anger;
　　I won't return to destroy Ephraim;
　for I am God and not a human being,
　　the holy one in your midst;
　I won't come in harsh judgment. (Hosea 11:8-9)

God is no mortal; the Lord remains faithful despite the people's unfaithfulness. That is the *hesed* of God. It's that divine hesed that Jesus comes to embody many centuries later.

The Love of Jesus Christ

In the life of Hosea, Gomer, and their children, we preview the justice that the Messiah in Jesus would ultimately bring by his birth, life, teaching, death, and resurrection. Justice, seen through the lens of *hesed*, is so much more than correcting what is wrong. In the life and teachings of Jesus, justice has a prophetic kingdom perspective, creating a window to grasp what ultimate salvation might look like: a glimpse into a time and place where even the lowest of us get not what we deserve, but rather what God offers: grace, love, and hope. Hope that this world, this life, isn't the end. Hope that amidst the struggle, there is a God. And hope that God hears our deepest cries and offers a faithfulness that extends far beyond what we imagine.

Maybe that's why Hosea was commanded to marry Gomer. Is it possible that their unorthodox marriage is a perfect and prophetic example of God? God doesn't judge us by our failures but rather sees us according to our capabilities. God chooses to see past our shortcomings and sees what even *we* might refuse to see or be unable to see.

Just as each marriage partner enters into covenant with the other, so has God made a covenant with creation. Israel's relationship with God, their *covenant* with God, was at stake. Limburg talks about the theme of breaking the covenant in Hosea 6:6-7 and 8:1-3. In both examples, Israel has knowledge of God, but knowledge alone is not enough—they must *actually know* God. Knowing God involves being in relationship with God; this is what the covenant was truly about. It wasn't just about keeping the rules; it was about interacting with God.[2]

When I read Hosea's story, I find myself angry on his behalf. It's like he has been dealt a bad hand in a game of cards with no way out. However, one of the beautiful aspects in Hosea's story is that, while we might find ourselves overwhelmed with anger and confusion, God isn't overwhelmed. Biblical scholars Bo Lim and Daniel Castelo write about the importance of maintaining the distinction between God and humanity: "For I am God and no mortal, the Holy One in your midst" (Hosea 11:9). In other words, *we are made in the image of God; God is not fashioned after us.*[3] Lim's and Castelo's point is thought-provoking and beautiful.

So, where in the story of Hosea and Gomer and children with the worst names ever might we find hints of the coming Messiah? Years later, God's ultimate love came to earth in Jesus Christ who was born near the city of Bethlehem. Jesus chose humble service rather than falling into the seduction of anger over love. Jesus showed us true power when he took a linen towel, wrapped it around his waist, and washed the disciples' feet, a task normally done by servants (John 13:1-7). Jesus, the Messiah, fully human and fully divine, washed his disciples' feet to give us another glimpse that the

Messiah came to serve in grace and love. Love finds strength in service rather than flexing power over the non-dominant. Hosea's marriage and life exemplify some of these same values. I can imagine the pain they might have gone through day after day. We have no record of Gomer's life before her marriage to Hosea. She is depicted in the Book of Hosea as a passive character who is primarily known for her nefarious occupation and the unfortunate names of her children. The story is messy, and many parts of this book don't sit easily with us. Why did he have to marry a prostitute? Weren't their children innocent? If so, why name them such horrible names? What happened to Gomer and her kids?

We don't know. What we do know is that Hosea used them as prophetic metaphors representing Israel and how they had dishonored God. In spite of Israel's disloyalty, God offers mercy, grace, and love. Hosea's marriage to Gomer provides an example of intentional presence. In the story, we see examples of God's *hesed*.

Maybe one value we can draw from this incredible story is the gift of sacredly sitting in the presence of God. That is, after all, what God desires as our part of the covenant relationship. God has been faithful to us, intentionally present with us. We can, and we must, respond in kind. We can be intentionally grounded and aware while looking for opportunities to act with justice and mercy. I wonder if the sacredness of sitting in the presence of one another is another way of offering ourselves as a gift of grace. There are certainly times when we need to act with integrity, to speak out against injustices in the world. Maybe then the wisdom and gift of the Holy Spirit begins to give us a taste of the kingdom to come.

Questions for Reflection and Discussion

1. What is the story behind your name?
2. What is the story of the names of the people you care for?

3. How do you hear God's calling in your life and faith community?
4. When have you felt God calling you to do something strange? How did you respond?
5. When have you felt betrayed by someone close to you? What metaphors would describe that betrayal?
6. What does loyalty mean to you? How do you express loyalty to others in your life?
7. How might you define God's *hesed*, God's faithfulness? How do you recognize it in your life today?

Prayer

Holy and Sacred One, thank you for all that you do and all that you have done in creation. You hear the cries of the marginalized and disenfranchised. Loving God, you who created us in your image, thank you for choosing us. Thank you for loving us. Each of us has a name, and your name is the name above all names, Jesus. Teach us today to love as you love, listen as you listen, and care as you care. Thanks be to you, O God. Amen

Focus for the Week

Take time to learn more about local nonprofit organizations near you that are seeking to provide justice for those who are vulnerable. Choose one way you can help make a real difference this week. As you do so, reflect on how this is an expression and embodiment of God's loyalty to you, your community, and those whom you serve. Strive to make your own actions a symbol of God's hesed.

Read the following Scriptures each day. Pause prayerfully before you read. Become aware of your breathing, of the ways you are drawn to this sacred moment, and of the ways you may be distracted. Offer all that is happening to God. Ask for God's guidance as you engage each of the readings.

Monday: Jonah 1:1-2
Tuesday: Jonah 1:3-5
Wednesday: Jonah 1:6-8
Thursday: Jonah 1:9-16
Friday: Jonah 1:17
Saturday: Jonah 1:1-17

1. From *Hosea-Micah: Interpretation*, by James Limburg (Westminster John Knox Press); page 4.

2. From *Hosea-Micah: Interpretation*, by James Limburg (Westminster John Knox Press); page 17.

3. From *Hosea*, by Bo H Lim and Daniel Castelo, The Two Horizons Old Testament Commentary (Eerdmans, 2015); page 174.

Nine Words That Changed Everything: Jonah

Scripture: Read Jonah 1:1-17

You are the LORD: whatever you want, you can do.
(Jonah 1:14)

I love ministry! When I was a senior in college, I was finishing my fourth year as a youth director for my local United Methodist church. I really loved working for the church. I loved talking with young people about faith, engaging in deep questions, and discussing how we can all grow in faith. I especially loved the time I spent with a group of guys for a weekly Bible study. They were active in the youth program I led, and it was a privilege to lead them in a Bible study group.

After college, I got a job as an intern for a large Presbyterian youth program in Boulder, Colorado. That magical year of ministry filled with adventures showed me that full-time ministry was satisfying and inspiring. With the skiing, rock climbing, and other adventures, I think I owed more money than I made! I lived in the basement of a gracious family that raised two Division I college football players. They initially tried to feed me the same way they fed their sons.

That was the year that I applied to Princeton Theological Seminary. I wanted to learn from people like Reverend Dr. Kenda Creasy Dean who shaped my understanding of ministry when I was a teenager. I wanted to study Hebrew, Greek, philosophy, and theologies that continue to shape our world today. I turned in my application and before I knew it, I got a letter in reply. I remember that day clearly. The moment I saw the thin envelope with the Princeton Theological Seminary seal, I grabbed the letter, ran down to the basement, and stood in the middle of my room. My heart was racing as I tore open the letter. Once I read the words that I had been accepted to graduate school, the power went out. The basement darkened, and my heart started to race even faster. I thought, *What could this mean? Is this a sign? If it is a sign, how do I interpret it?*

The church where I was working had invited me to come back another year, which was tempting. I was having such a great time there. But seminary was an exciting idea; I remembered reading in Matthew 3 about how John the Baptist lived in the wild and ate locusts and wild honey. Was Princeton, New Jersey, supposed to be my desert?

While the power was out for hours, I went to my favorite coffee shop to consider what to do. Deep down I feared what life as a pastor could actually be like. I struggled over living on the East coast for several years. Ultimately, I didn't know if this was my calling or not. I didn't know what to do.

So, what was my decision? I chose a third option. I decided to delay my decision, and in essence, I ran. I wrote a letter to delay my enrollment another year. I packed up my bags, and I moved back home to live with my parents. I took the first decent job I could find and started working at AT&T Wireless in a place I had never heard of. For the next year of my life, I worked just a handful of miles from where I am serving as I write this book. At first the work was fun, exciting, and new. Soon, it became tedious, monotonous, and unfulfilling.

My new profession was in telemarketing. I was a part of a team that focused on customer retention. If a customer used more than fifty percent of his or her calling plan, my job was to offer the customer a better rate. We used an automated system that dialed people on their personal cell phones so that I could speak with them to make the offer. This was around the year 2000 when the only people calling cell phones were a select few friends. I remember sitting on the phone, trying to convince customers that I wasn't a con artist and that I got their personal cell phone number legitimately. One day, I called a famous, retired professional basketball player from Seattle. It took me several moments to realize who I was talking to; when I did, I felt sheepish as I went through my scripted lines. That one call was the highlight of a year's worth of calling because he was a childhood hero of mine.

That year had many memorable moments. I resumed my Bible study with the same guys I met with before I moved to Colorado. During one of our weekly meetings, one of the guys said, "DJ, you could be doing this for a living. You're sitting on a winning lottery ticket to go back to school and you just won't cash it! What are you doing?"

The truth behind his words was exactly what I needed to hear. I had spent a whole year spinning my wheels trying to convince myself that seminary was not my calling. I had found little joy or satisfaction in my work, but I had tried to convince myself that it was my calling. His words were exactly what I needed to hear to finally answer God's call to go to seminary.

In this chapter, we continue our journey to the empty cross and empty grave through the eyes of Jonah, who, in my opinion, is probably the worst prophet. Jonah also ran from his calling, and needed more than a little convincing to undertake the task for which God commissioned him. With four short chapters (just forty-eight verses), the book is worth reading in one sitting.

Running From God

Check out the first few words in Jonah 1:1. Jonah is identified "Amittai's son." *Amittai* is a name derived from the Hebrew root that means "to be faithful."[1] This name turns out to be ironic because of what we soon discover about Jonah's nature. Jonah was not faithful throughout this book. In verse 2, Jonah hears God's calling: "Get up and go to Nineveh, that great city, and cry out against it, for their evil has come to my attention." God tells Jonah to go among the Israelites' mortal enemies, to the capital of the Assyrian empire, Nineveh.[2] It was the Assyrian empire that conquered and destroyed the northern kingdom of Israel in 722 BC, exiling much of its population in the same way that Babylon would conquer Judah more than a century later. God is telling Jonah to preach to his enemies. What does Jonah do? He starts running the opposite direction! Jonah is no hero. The son of Amittai, "to be faithful," is not an example of a faithful servant.

Jonah's name is most commonly translated as "dove." In Genesis 8, you might recall, Noah sent a raven and a dove to look for dry land after the great Flood. The dove brought back an olive leaf, a sign of hope that humanity could rebuild (Genesis 8:11). The dove is also the sign of the Holy Spirit descending upon Jesus when he was baptized (Matthew 3:13-17; Mark 1:9-11; Luke 3:21-22). The dove is a symbol of the Holy Spirit who will draw people together. Maybe Jonah's name, the Dove, was also meant to be ironic. His actions in these four chapters of the book named after him do not resemble the work of doves in Scripture. Instead, he's the reluctant, self-centered prophet who doesn't draw people together.

God tells Jonah to preach to the Ninevites: "Get up and go to Nineveh, that great city, and cry out against it, for their evil has come to my attention" (Jonah 1:1). In response, Jonah pulls a 180-degree turn and goes the opposite direction. He jumps on a nearby boat headed toward Tarshish, away from Nineveh and "away from the LORD" (1:3). Scripture tells us that a nasty storm rocked the boat, scaring everyone on board except Jonah. Why? Because Jonah was in a deep sleep in the hold of the ship (1:5).

Eventually, Jonah confessed to the men on the boat that he was responsible for their horrible situation. Jonah told them, "I'm a Hebrew. I worship the LORD, the God of heaven—who made the sea and the dry land" (1:9). When they asked what they should do to make the seas calm again, he said, "Pick me up and hurl me into the sea! Then the sea will become calm around you. I know it's my fault that this great storm has come upon you" (1:12). Was Jonah trying to die? Did he want to avoid going to Nineveh so badly that he would take his chances in the deep and raging sea? Jonah didn't ask to be saved. He just asked to be tossed in the sea. To die. The sailors prayed to the LORD, hurled Jonah into the sea, and the sea became calm (1:13-15). Despite Jonah's lack of desire to follow his calling from God, despite his deep sleep and his confession, when the seas calmed all the people on the boat began to worship his God (1:16).

In Jonah 1:17, the LORD provided a great fish to swallow Jonah. A lot of debate surrounds Jonah surviving three days and nights in a large fish. How is this possible, and what sort of creature was it? We typically imagine a whale, though the Hebrew is best translated as "large fish" or "great fish." The Septuagint, the primary Greek translation of the Hebrew Scriptures, uses a word meaning "sea monster." Regardless of what kind of creature it was, it saved Jonah's life. If the creature hadn't swallowed him, Jonah would have drowned in the sea. And finally, in the deep belly of the great fish, Jonah had a change of heart. He prayed and declared "Deliverance belongs to the LORD!" (Jonah 2:9). By the end of Chapter 2, the fish spewed Jonah out onto dry land.

In Matthew 12:40, Jesus compared his three days in the grave to Jonah's three days in the belly of a fish. Someday, I'll be excited to ask Jesus why he compared his time in the grave to Jonah's time in the belly of a fish. Jonah was running from his calling while Jesus chose to fulfill his.

Nine Words

Jonah's time in the fish leads him to a change of heart, so that when God again tells him to go to Nineveh, Jonah does so (Jonah 3:1-3). God tells Jonah to "declare against it the proclamation that I am commanding you" (3:2). It is a short proclamation. Abraham Lincoln's famous Gettysburg address was short, only about 270 words (less than 3 minutes).[3] Jonah has Abraham Lincoln beat by a long shot. In Jonah 3:4, the prophet walked into Nineveh and dropped a nine-word sermon. Only nine words: "Just forty days more and Nineveh will be overthrown!" (In the original Hebrew it's even shorter, only five words!) Jonah delivered nine words and then decided he'd fulfilled the LORD's command. His work was done. Jonah then went outside the city to watch it burn to the ground. But instead, the entire city repented. Check out 3:5-9. The whole city fasted and mourned and called upon God. The king repented. Even their animals wore sackcloth as they repented. Jonah 4:11 tells us that one hundred and twenty thousand people repented on the basis of Jonah's words. And God saw their repentance and spared the city of Nineveh (3:10). It was a nine-word sermon, but those nine words changed everything.

How does our reluctant prophet respond when his nine-word sermon leads to repentance and the people of Ninevah are not destroyed? Does he waive his arms in triumph? Does he take a victory lap? No. Jonah is *not* happy (Jonah 4:1-3). Jonah wanted to witness death and destruction, but instead the Ninevites repented. The king, the people, the animals wore sackcloth and showed signs of real contrition. Jonah's nine-word sermon moved a whole city—a great city—to repentance, and God spared the city and its people. In terms of results, Jonah was the most successful prophet of all time. And he was angry about the outcome.

Grace for One's Enemies

We don't know many details about the Ninevites in this story. We don't know any of their names. We can safely deduce that this story is more about Jonah and God than about the people on the boat during a storm or even a city of people repenting. We do know, however, that God's mind is changed; God decides to not punish the Ninevites after all. This isn't the only time God's mind is changed. In Exodus 32, the Hebrew people melted their gold to make metal cows to worship while waiting for Moses to bring the Ten Commandments from God on Mt. Sinai. God wanted to devour the people, but Moses changed God's mind (Exodus 32:10-14). Perhaps we can learn something by comparing these two stories in which God's mind was changed.

Much debate surrounds the Book of Jonah. I like to call these debates theological wrinkles. Theological wrinkles are pieces of Scripture that seem out of place. Just like a bad wrinkle on a shirt, your eye is naturally drawn to it because it seems out of place. When studying the Bible, I like to find these wrinkles and unfold them. One big wrinkle in Jonah's story has to do with the Assyrians. God cares about the same people who are responsible for destroying his people (the Northern Kingdom) in 722 BC. God calls Jonah to preach to them. As a result, they repent! Contrast the nameless, faceless one hundred twenty thousand Assyrians in Nineveh to the stories of the Hebrew people who do not repent. The Hebrew people were saved from slavery in Egypt. They witnessed the plagues. The sea parted as Pharaoh's army chased them. Still they betrayed God. Despite having Moses as their leader and experiencing all of the miracles, the Hebrew people still turned to their own devices, choosing to worship gold and metal. The story of Jonah is the story of foreigners, enemies even, who respond to God faithfully, and the Israelite prophet who resents God for it. It's about the startling, scandalous reality that God's grace really does extend to all people.

God's grace, God's plan for salvation, was always intended to be shared with all of creation. Long before Jesus walked this earth, stories like the repentance of the Ninevites give us a glimpse of God who loves everyone as well as the chosen people.

It's simply amazing how God used a reluctant prophet who really didn't want to preach to his worst enemies.

Instead Jonah would have rather run away, would have rather drowned in the sea. It took him three days in the belly of a great fish to come around, and even then he preached the world's worst sermon even though he didn't really want to. He was a prophet who, even after witnessing the success of his sermon, sulked on the outskirts of town because the death and destruction he was hoping for never came to fruition. Jonah is angry with God: "Come on, LORD! Wasn't this precisely my point when I was back in my own land? This is why I fled to Tarshish earlier! I know that you are a merciful and compassionate God, very patient, full of faithful love, and willing not to destroy" (Jonah 4:2). Despite Jonah being possibly the worst prophet in the Bible, God still chose to use him and reach many lives.

God chose to continue teaching Jonah as well. When Jonah expressed his anger about the preservation of Nineveh, God sent a plant to provide shade for him. But the next day, God sent a worm to destroy the plant, so that Jonah was exposed to the heat once again. God then invited Jonah to consider his response to the plant's demise. If Jonah could pity the plant, isn't it fitting that God should have pity on Nineveh and all its inhabitants? Like many stories in the Bible, this one is left open-ended; we don't know Jonah's response. What's clear, though, is that God was trying to teach Jonah that God's love encompasses all people, even Jonah's enemies.

God's Love and Justice Encompasses All

The story of Jonah foreshadows the coming of the Messiah. Jesus came to the earth and offered love and grace to all people, even those that no one believed could deserve it. Tax collectors, prostitutes, the loathsome, and the lonely were all loved by Jesus. And his love by our standards simply doesn't make sense when we consider that this love is available to even our enemies. We follow a God whose justice, mercy, and love compels us to love even those we might hate the most. We live in a time and a place where many churches and institutions are known for what or who they stand against rather than who and what they stand for. Maybe it's time for us to focus on God who has always stood for all. All means all. You, me, the stranger across the street, the coworker or classmate who gets under our skin, the politician, the lobbyist, and even that family member you struggle with most.

There is a time when truth needs to be spoken in a prophetic and fearless way. There is also a time when we need to focus on what we believe in rather than what we do not agree with. That, too, can be prophetic. Jonah's nine simple words changed a city. How are you being called to be a prophet through your actions and words? My prayer for you this week is that you take God's calling in your life seriously and look for opportunities to move into action.

God used a reluctant prophet whose nine-word sermon made a difference to Ninevah and revealed the nature of God. One of my favorite parts about Jonah's story is that God is patient with Jonah too. God engages with him right where he is; even when Jonah sits outside the city to pout, God continues to show Jonah love and mercy and teaches Jonah about a compassion that embraces even the enemy. "Yet for my part, can't I pity Nineveh, that great city, in which there are more than one hundred twenty thousand people who can't tell their right hand from their left, and also many animals?" (Jonah 4:11). This is the wind in Jonah's wilderness, the affirmation that God has power over all creation and cares for all creation. God delivers. God saves, even the enemy. This is the foreshadowing of God's actions through Jesus.

The kingdom is coming; if God can use people like Jonah to change a boat of people and to change the lives of one hundred twenty thousand people with nine simple words, where is God calling us? Where is God calling you? Who are the people you are struggling with the most? Where is God calling you to stand prophetically and say that God's love is greater than this moment and this time?

The kingdom is coming. How will you respond?

53

Questions for Reflection and Discussion

1. Where did you experience God today'?
2. How is Jonah's story similar to your life today?
3. When have you felt a calling from God to do something uncomfortable?
4. What does obedience mean to you regarding discipleship?
5. What did it mean to be a prophet in Jonah's time?
6. What does it mean to be a prophet today?
7. Who do you struggle to affirm and recognize as a recipient of God's love, grace, and forgiveness? How does your attitude toward them need to change?
8. What insights do you gain from Jonah about how you might show God's love to them?

Prayer

Loving God, your way and your will are far beyond our ways, our will, and our desires. Thank you for people like Jonah who remind us of this through his life, through his reluctance, and especially through the ways you worked through the best of him while honoring his struggles. The Kingdom is coming, and your grace is amazing and transformative. Thank you for the ways we can begin to practice and live into this amazing grace. Come Holy Spirit come. Amen.

Focus for the Week

How are you called to be a prophet through your actions and words? Take time to reflect seriously on God's calling in your life and look for opportunities this week to move into action.

Read the following Scriptures each day. Pause prayerfully before you read. Become aware of your breathing, of the ways you are drawn to this sacred moment, and of the ways you may be distracted. Offer all that is happening to God. Ask for God's guidance as you engage each of the readings.

Monday: Job 1:6-8
Tuesday: Job 1:9-12
Wednesday: Job 1:13-15
Thursday: Job 1:16-17
Friday: Job 1:18-19
Saturday: Job 1:6-22

1. From *www.workingpreacher.org/preaching.aspx?commentary_id=1445*. Accessed 7 October 2016.

2. From *www.workingpreacher.org/preaching.aspx?commentary_id=2347*. Accessed 7 October 2016.

3. The text of the five copies of the speech can be accessed online at: *www.abrahamlincolnonline.org/lincoln/speeches/gettysburg.htm*. Accessed 7 October 2016.

Present in the Waiting: Job

Scripture: Read Job 1:6-22

The LORD has given; the LORD has taken; bless the LORD's name. (Job 1:21)

OK, I know what you are going to say. Job isn't a prophet. Here you are reading a book on the prophets and their vision of justice, and all of a sudden you arrive at Chapter 4 and discover a meditation on Job. "Don't get me wrong," you might say, "I like Job just fine. But he isn't a prophet." You are undoubtedly correct. Job isn't a prophet. I make no attempt to pretend that he is. I can only ask your forgiveness and forge ahead, hoping that you'll stick with me for this chapter too.

Perhaps it will help if I tell you that my reason for including Job is what this book communicates to us about *waiting*. Job suffers much, as we're going to see, and he struggles to understand why bad things happen and what they mean. Job's friends attempt to do the same, and in the process they illustrate for us the pitfalls of trying to do too much, to say too much, rather than simply waiting and trusting God, seeking to be faithful without having all the answers. How can we be present in the waiting? That is a key question of the Book of Job.

It's also a key question for us as we consider the Hebrew prophets, their message of justice, and their fulfillment in Jesus. The visions of which the prophets spoke would be fulfilled only at a much later date than when they were revealed. Frequently, the people had to experience suffering and try to make sense of it in the meantime, without having full knowledge of what was coming. They felt only a wind in the wilderness, sometimes only a light breeze, and nothing more. How could they be present in the waiting, in the meantime, when the prophecies had been uttered but the One they spoke of was still to come?

As we journey on toward Palm Sunday, the crucifixion of Jesus, and the Resurrection on Easter Sunday, we too need a lesson in how to be present in the waiting. It remains true that the justice Jesus came to usher in often feels a long way off. It remains true that in between the Crucifixion on Friday and the Resurrection on Sunday there is a Saturday of waiting without all the answers or a sense of what it all means. And so we turn to Job to help us wait, to be present and faithful in the meantime. Job is not a prophet. But Job is one of us.

Not If, But When

The best part of a scary movie is when I know something is going to happen. The music and the anticipation swell, and I know something will happen; I believe something will happen. You know what I'm talking about. Remember the *Jaws* soundtrack? Remember the haunting music foreshadowing the potential demise of the hopeless hero desperately swimming to shore while the shark's fin stalks him in the background? We can anticipate what will happen, and it builds the suspense. Knowing what's about to happen enhances the movie experience.

Sometimes, though, knowing too much makes things worse. I took twenty weeks to prepare for my first marathon. And every time I trained, I was consumed by the idea of "hitting the wall." One of my friends who is a competitive runner said, "DJ, when it comes to running 26.2 miles, it's not a matter of *if* you hit a wall and want to give up; it's a matter of *when*." I remember hitting my wall. I was about twenty-three miles into the marathon when I realized that this was farther than I had ever run. Not a second later, the person directly in front of me collapsed. Another person collapsed shortly after that. My elated spirit evaporated as I became aware of the ache in my knees, the pain in my feet, and my dwindling energy. I wondered if I could finish the marathon—forget about my target goal of breaking the four-hour mark. Half a mile later, my focus shifted to an internal chant: "One foot in front of another! Left-foot, right-foot; one foot in front of another! Left foot, right foot." The wall came, and that's what I had to do to get past it. It wasn't the *if*; it was the *when*. Waiting for the wall to hit me was hard. But actively waiting, persevering, through the experience of hitting the wall so I could finish the marathon was even harder. I had to be present in the waiting, aware and actively engaged the whole time.

That kind of waiting—being present in the waiting—is especially hard to do. I hope that you are able to regularly spend quality time with people you love. I pray that you are able to take a break from work, school, or other obligations to slow down and really catch your breath this Lenten season. It seems that being present in the waiting is getting harder and harder to do. While being intentionally present focuses in the moment, being present in the waiting means being aware and engaged while waiting in this Lenten season for Easter.

How might you be present in the waiting?" Perhaps you might begin by looking around while standing in line at the grocery store, or taking in your surroundings at a stop light. How many people do you see? What are your fellow humans doing as they wait? In those few seconds of waiting, do they become grounded in that moment rather than waiting for the seconds to tick by? Perhaps you might take this opportunity to consider the holes we are in as we wait for God's kingdom to come—to take notice of your surroundings and your circumstances, and how God might deliver us from those things that threaten our well-being.

We have access to information like no other previous generation. From smartphones to the World Wide Web, we can search any question that occurs to us. We have access to countless opinions and facts. But sometimes, knowing too much and not knowing what to do with all information can be challenging. It can prevent us from being present in the waiting. Whenever I am waiting line, I find myself automatically pulling out my phone to check for any messages and check out my social media sites. I can't remember when I started this habit of checking my phone when I have a few spare seconds. Maybe it was when I noticed other people checking their phones. Maybe it's because I grew up in a place where people didn't make eye contact with strangers, so I didn't know what else to do with myself. I can't really remember what people did to kill time before cell phones. I remember that there was a day when not everyone had their own cell phone. I just can't remember how we passed the time.

Job

The Scripture reading in this chapter focuses on a man named Job who had to wait. The Book of Job is dense; even the first few chapters are packed. Job begins with God and a character called the Adversary placing a bet. The Adversary argues that Job is devoted to God because God has blessed Job. To prove his point, the Adversary asks God's permission to strip away all of the blessings Job enjoys. The bet is placed. Will Job continue to be blameless and righteous when stripped bare of everything he owns and loves, or will he denounce God?

So, the bet is on! Job receives four horrific messages in one day (Job 1:13-19). Have you ever had one of those days that you just you need to be over? Job is plagued by invaders and natural disasters; he loses livestock, servants, and even his children. This story of Job is so rich and profound because it's complex and isn't a book that can be skimped though. God doesn't always come across as compassionate and gracious in every verse. Something unique in this story is that Job is depicted as a non-Hebrew person. The Old Testament (also known as the Hebrew Scriptures) is full of stories of the Hebrew people; yet, here we have this critical piece of wisdom that features a group other than the Hebrew people. No one really seems to know exactly when this story was written, though it may have been written sometime between the sixth and fourth centuries BC. It deals too much with universal human questions to permit any definitive dating.

So, what can we learn from Job's story? Is this divine lesson about suffering? Justice? piety? righteousness? The nature of God? The problem of evil? If God is a good God, how can God permit what happened to Job and his family? We know that this is a story of a man who endures some of the worst circumstances a person might imagine.

An essential question I have when studying the Book of Job is "Why?" Why would a good God allow such horrible things to happen? Asking why is an essential building block of faith. The wrestling, the struggling, the discernment is where faith takes hold. This, I think, is where waiting plays a key role. If we take a closer look at the story, we can see that everyone in it is waiting. The Adversary is waiting for Job to curse God. God is waiting for Job to remain faithful. Later in the story, Job's friends are waiting for Job's misery to end. And Job himself is waiting on an answer from God about why such suffering has come upon him. Everyone seems to be waiting for the page of history to turn and this horrible chapter to end. There is power in waiting, and there is truth in asking, "Are you there, God?"

Are You There, God?

People all around the world are asking, "Are you there, God?" For some, for many, maybe for you, this is *the* question in Lent. Jesus may have been born in a different generation, but how is he relevant in today's world with folks struggling in the here and now? So many natural and unnatural disasters happen in our world and, far too often, we as a church respond with pithy sentences or with theology that damages more than it heals. What happens when churchy words and sayings sound hollow?

"God is large and in charge!" This motto was a favorite of a minister where I attended church in college. For years, I loved this statement; I lived by it. I recited it when tragedy happened. It felt right. We worship a God who is large and in charge! It felt bold and brave. The motto worked for me for a long time, until I went deeper. If God was really in charge of everything, if God directly manipulates every single act, does this large-and-in-charge God who is the Creator choose that some would suffer more than others? How or why would God allow such horrible things to happen? How do we reconcile our faith with a "large-and-in-charge" God who seems to seek revenge in Scripture and commands the genocide of people, such as we see in the Books of Deuteronomy and Joshua? That seemed to be incredibly inconsistent with the God of compassion and grace who I read about in other parts of Scripture. Does God will every single act of good and bad for some unknown purpose?

The question I see posed by the Book of Job, "Are you there, God?" is much more true to the human experience and the complexity of life. At times, life does feel as if the answer to this question might really be no. The hope that we have as Christians involves a lot of waiting, and being present in the waiting, while we wrestle as Job does with uncertainty.

Christians believe that we are created in the image of God and that we are blessed with the free will to choose our own actions, whether right or wrong. We know that the choices of others or our own choices broadly affect those around us. We live in a world that is full of holes. We believe that Jesus lived, taught, loved, died, and rose again. We know why we celebrate the birth of the Christ at Christmas, and we know why Easter matters. One translation of the word *peace* in the

Hebrew language is wholeness. We believe that there will be a day when all will be made whole through Jesus—a day when peace is on earth and reigns throughout earth. But that day hasn't happened yet, so we wait.

Often we sense something sacred in being present in the waiting. The sacredness doesn't mean it's an easy wait, just like waiting in line and being intentionally present doesn't often come naturally. Being present in the waiting is a spiritual discipline. As we move deeper into this season of Lent, I find it helpful for us to stop and consider the nature of God, and ultimately we will get a glimpse of the Messiah to come.

One of my favorite theologians is Dietrich Bonhoeffer. He was born in 1906 and was a politically active pastor and seminary professor in Germany during World War II. Bonhoeffer wrote about Advent in a way that describes what waiting is all about during the season of Lent. He says, "Advent can be celebrated only by those whose souls give them no peace, who know that they are poor and incomplete, and who sense something of the greatness that is supposed to come."[1] He was describing the season of Advent, a season of waiting in the Christian year. But I think his words apply equally well to the kind of waiting we do in Lent. Being present in the waiting doesn't mean being lonely. It doesn't mean being blissfully ignorant or sitting idly. Rather, being present, becoming rooted in the now, forces us to become aware of our surroundings. We slow down enough to acknowledge the presence of struggles and joys in our lives as we encounter the Sacred One who is present with us in the now.

Instead of reciting "God is large and in charge!" I find myself responding to tragedies and moments of struggle in another ways. I often begin with "Lord in your mercy," then I move to God's presence or ask, "Are you there, God?" I find that this engagement with God feels very authentic and honest. This approach invites an exploration and study rather than blanketing the tragedy in cliché.

Asking the Hard Questions

Mary Oliver is a Pulitzer Prize-winning poet. One of her poems in particular, *The Summer Day*, speaks to my heart. I encourage you to look it up and read it, either in a book or online. It can be accessed at the Library of Congress website (*www.loc.gov/poetry/180/133.html*). The poem ends with the following: "Tell me, what is it you plan to do with your one wild and precious life?" In our lives, we can wait next to one another in the lines we are in. We can pull out our cell phones and find ways to pass the time, or we can choose to take advantage of this one wild and precious life. We can take this life, opportunities that are presented daily before us, and broaden our perspective to what will be in Jesus.

In light of this insightful question, I want to continue this chapter with a confession. I have a growing list of unanswered questions that I tuck away in a special place in my heart. This list contains mostly faith-based questions that I have about God. Although the list grows, it does not diminish my understanding of (and desire to understand) the living God. These tucked-away questions are not bottled up somewhere, never to be uncovered. I am not afraid of them. They reside close to my heart.

When I ponder a question that is securely tucked away, it only leads to more questions. Occasionally, rarely, God answers one of them. Sometimes I share them with other Christians; other times, I explore them with people who are not Christians. And sometimes I debate and argue them with God. As I read through Scripture, I know God is no stranger to people with questions. It is how we are supposed to be. How else are we supposed to grow? These questions keep my faith journey a relationship with the risen Christ, not a prescribed faith checklist. This is the posture our faith must take, while we wait for the justice of God revealed in Jesus Christ to come to fulfillment.

As a college student, I led a weekly Bible study for high school students. I had gone to church my whole life, and felt very confident that teaching a Bible study was something I was well qualified for. I went to a Christian bookstore and bought a popular Bible study book that looked cool. The lessons weren't too long and I wouldn't have to prepare too much. I assumed that anything I bought at a Christian bookstore would be good. Boy, was I wrong.

As soon as we started the lessons, the group started asking questions that I could not answer. "Does the Bible really say that?" "If God really loves everyone, how come some people have terrible things happen to them?" I tried to field their questions, feeling that it was my duty to have answers. But I felt terrible the whole time because I knew I was just making stuff up. My experience with this study was a big reason I went to seminary. I desired a period of time in my life when I could study, debate, and discuss theology and Scripture in a setting that taught me how to think about and express my faith in a reflective and responsible way.

One of the functions of church is just that. The time on Sunday morning is a time when we can ask existing questions, find new questions, and ponder the living God. I appreciate seasons like Lent because God is teaching us, through community and personal study, that God is present with us. God listens, engages, and is deeply involved in all of creation. As we go deeper into the season of Lent, we approach Palm Sunday and, shortly afterward, Maundy Thursday and Good Friday. God is present with us even then, especially then, as we remember Christ's betrayal, suffering, and death.

May your whole self be rooted in the present as we wait, anticipate, and prepare together. May you know that we worship God who is able to handle your questions. May we boldly ask where God is in all that's good and all that's wrong in our world. We worship God who is more than capable of handling our questions and our struggles, even when we question and struggle with God. May this be a time when we are grounded in the here and now while knowing, believing, and working for a kingdom that we know is possible. Amen.

Questions for Reflection and Discussion

1. Which parts of Job's story do you resonate with most in this season of your life?
2. What does it mean to be present in the waiting?
3. How do you respond in faith during times of tragedy?
4. What is it you plan to do with your one wild and precious life?
5. What hard questions do you struggle with?
6. How does this struggle affect your relationship with God, positively and negatively?

Prayer

Thank you, Lord Jesus, for hearing our prayers. Thank you for hearing the cry of creation. Thank you for being present as we wait attentively for you. Thank you for your patience. In the midst of this Lenten time, give us this day our daily portion of patience, love, and grace. May we taste and see and know that you are God. Amen.

Focus for the Week

Invest 15 minutes each day to engaging in the news, whatever method you prefer. While you read the news, recite to yourself, "I am present in the waiting." Look for opportunities to respond and engage from a faith-based perspective. How is God calling you to be present in waiting for the Kingdom that is coming?

Read the following Scriptures each day. Pause prayerfully before you read. Become aware of your breathing, of the ways you are drawn to this sacred moment, and of the ways you may be distracted. Offer all that is happening to God. Ask for God's guidance as you engage each of the readings.

Monday: Zechariah 9:9-10
Tuesday: Matthew 21:1-3
Wednesday: Matthew 21:4-7
Thursday: Matthew 21:8-9
Friday: Matthew 21:10-11
Saturday: Zechariah 9:9-10

1. From *God Is In the Manger: Reflections on Advent and Christmas,* by Dietrich Bonhoeffer; edited by Jana Reiss; translated by O. C. Dean, Jr. (Westminster John Knox Press, 2010); page 6.

Matthew Fox
Cosmic Christ

1 Scripture
*
2 Reason
3 Experience
4 Tradition

A Taste of the Good Life: Zechariah

Scripture: Read Zechariah 9:9-10 and Matthew 21:1-17

Look, your king will come to you.
  He is righteous and victorious.
  He is humble and riding on an ass,
    on a colt, the offspring of a donkey.
                    (Zechariah 9:9)

Have you read the series *The Chronicles of Narnia*? This series was written in the 1950s by C. S. Lewis, writer, academic, and apologist, who was the chair of medieval and Renaissance literature at Cambridge.[1] This series of seven books is rich in theology. Different characters face unique challenges. One character is present in all books and pulls all of the stories together: The great and powerful Aslan, who is not tame but is always good.

One book I particularly love is *The Lion, the Witch, and the Wardrobe*, the first book in the series. In it, Lewis tells the story of four siblings who discover the land of Narnia by entering the world through a magical wardrobe. The children speak at one point with local Narnian creatures Mr. and Mrs. Beaver about Aslan, the King of Narnia. The children heard stories about the powerful Aslan, but were unsure what to make of him. The children assumed Aslan was a man and quickly found out that he was a great lion. "Then he isn't safe?" asked Lucy, one of the children. Mr. Beaver replied, "Safe? . . . don't you hear what Mrs. Beaver tells you? Who said anything about safe? 'Course he isn't safe. But he's good. He's the King, I tell you." Later in the book, we read another warning from Mr. Beaver. "He'll be coming and going' he had said. 'One day you'll see him and another you won't. He doesn't like being tied down—and of course he has other countries to attend to. It's quite all right. He'll often drop in. Only you mustn't press him. He's wild you know. Not like a *tame* lion."[2]

Not tame. According to Merriam-Webster's dictionary, one way of defining the word *tame* is "Not wild: trained to obey people."[3]

Everyone knew that all would be well when Aslan arrived. And they knew that Aslan was not a tame lion. They knew that he was wild, but full of grace; that he was good, but not safe. Aslan was not a predictable lion. He wasn't at the Narnians' beck and call, nor was he readily available to the visiting children. Yet even when the characters of Narnia didn't fully understand the outcome of events, he was always working toward goodness and grace.

Jesus Isn't Tame

It's too easy to talk about God without engaging in who God truly is—who Jesus, fully human and fully God, was on earth and who he is today. We often refer to God or to Jesus in much the same way that a fashion label is mentioned on the red carpet. After a sports victory, we might bring up Jesus as if we knew his will was to create winners and losers. Ultimately, on some of our worst days, we equate Jesus to a super celebrity or a powerful prophet of his time and we see him as being safe and predictable. We celebrate the prophecy that our God is coming to us (Zechariah 9), not pausing to think that God's visit might be frightening and challenging rather than something we welcome. We fondly claim that Jesus is full of grace and love while forgetting that he turned over the money tables (Matthew 21). What we often get in the media is an image of Jesus that pales in comparison to the Jesus we read about in the Scriptures.

But Jesus is not someone we can train or manipulate. We know that Jesus is good, just, and full of grace. But Jesus was hardly predictable. He was never *just* fully human. He was also fully divine. Jesus was ever present and part of the triune God. He turned over tables in worship places; he challenged the status quo; he healed on days when he wasn't supposed to; he drank wine, partied with the people, and turned his back on the religious elite by choosing to eat with those whom the religious leaders rejected. This Jesus was far from predictable. He was good, but he wasn't safe. He wasn't tame.

One example of a tame and predictable Jesus comes from a theology called the prosperity gospel. Prosperity gospel is a theology steeped in the belief that God wants us to be blessed—usually financially blessed. The problem with theology that connects personal success to God's blessing is that our theology may become shallow and fragile. This is especially true in times when life becomes challenging. Is God purposely choosing to hurt us if we do not experience prosperity? I can understand how this might happen. It's easy to try to make Jesus obedient to us instead of trying to be obedient to him. We package him up into a safe and predictable figure, marketable to the masses. But Jesus is not safe, predictable, or tame.

Zechariah and Palm Sunday

Nowhere is Jesus' wild, untame nature on display more clearly than in his procession to Jerusalem on Palm Sunday, a week before he is crucified. Jesus enters Jerusalem to the praise and excitement of large crowds, then goes to the Temple and causes a major disturbance by throwing out those who are buying and selling.

In Matthew's Gospel, Jesus rides into Jerusalem on a very specific animal. Well, it's really two animals: a donkey and a colt (Matthew 21:1-7). Matthew makes clear that these animals represent the messianic fulfillment of the Hebrew Scriptures: Zechariah 9:9 associates the king who will come with both the donkey and the colt:

Look, your king will come to you.
 He is righteous and victorious.
 He is humble and riding on an ass,
  on a colt, the offspring of a donkey.

Matthew 21:4-5 quotes Zechariah as a way to describe Jesus' entry into Jerusalem as a fulfillment of Zechariah's prophecy.

It's important to recognize that Jesus specifically instructed his disciples to bring these animals to him for the purpose of his entry into Jerusalem (Matthew 21:1-3).

[1]When they approached Jerusalem and came to Bethphage on the Mount of Olives, Jesus gave two disciples a task. [2] He said to them, "Go into the village over there. As soon as you enter, you will find a donkey tied up and a colt with it. Untie them and bring them to me. [3] If anybody says anything to you, say that the Lord needs it." He sent them off right away.

In their book *The Last Week,* Marcus Borg and John Dominic Crossan call this ride a "prearranged counter-procession."[4] Jesus' entry into Jerusalem stood in contrast to that of Pontius Pilate, the Roman governor of Jerusalem. Borg and Crossan write, "Jesus's procession deliberately countered what was happening on the other side of the city. Pilate's procession embodied the power, glory, and violence of the empire that ruled the world. Jesus's procession embodied an alternative vision, the kingdom of God."[5] Matthew's distinctive and emphatic assertion that Jesus borrows two animals for his entry into Jerusalem exemplifies Zechariah's prophecy in Zechariah 9:9, that the coming king would be both "powerful and humble."[6]

The name Zechariah means "the LORD remembered." He is widely considered the key prophet of the postexilic time. Postexilic time is the period when the people of Judah would return from Babylon. Zechariah's pedigree was outstanding: Zechariah's grandfather, Iddo, was the head of one of the twelve priestly families of Israel.[7] During the time of restoration, 520–518 BC, Zechariah encouraged the Hebrew people to rebuild the house of the Lord, get their lives to return to righteous living with God, and to live their lives anticipating God's reign.

The prophet Zechariah served his people as they slowly pulled their lives back together after years of oppression. In doing so, he continued to remind them that salvation would not arrive according to their terms and expectations. Instead, humble service would usher in the kingdom of God.

Overturning Expectations

All four Gospels have stories of crowds that gathered around Jesus as he entered Jerusalem on Palm Sunday in fulfillment of this prophecy from Zechariah. According to Luke 19:29-40, the palm processional is led by Jesus' disciples. Instead of nameless and faceless crowds, the people who spread their clothes on the road and sang praises to God were Jesus' closest friends. We read about a different kind of crowd in John Chapter 12. They came to see Jesus who had just recently raised Lazarus from the dead (See John 11; 12:17). The people in the crowd heard that there was a man who was once dead for days and now was alive. They heard about the man who raised him from the dead was also coming to Jerusalem. In Matthew 21 and Mark 11, Jesus is greeted by large crowds, and we have no idea who is in the crowd. Matthew focuses on the energy surrounding Jesus' entry: As the city asked, "Who is this?" the crowd answered, "It's the prophet, Jesus, from Nazareth in Galilee." And the crowd shouted and sang, "*Hosanna* to the Son of David! *Blessings on the one who comes in the name of the Lord! Hosanna* in the highest!" I wonder if the people who shouted "Hosanna" are the same people that would shout "Crucify him! Crucify him!" later that week. How could their glee turn to such murderous thoughts so quickly?

We can start to answer this question by understanding the people's expectations about who Jesus was and what he was going to do. Take the palm leaves, for example. Palm leaves were a symbol of military victory, and they had been used to celebrate the victory of Judas "the Hammer" Maccabeus, who led the Jews to victory over their Greek rulers more than a hundred years before Jesus was born. In 164 BC, Judas Maccabaeus defeated the foreigners, who had desecrated the Temple by setting up an altar to Zeus and offering unclean animals upon it. After defeating the Greeks in battle, Judas and his people cleansed the Temple and restored the sacred worship space. According to the apocryphal Book of 2 Maccabees, the Jews celebrated this victory and the restoration of the Temple by palm fronds and branches (2 Maccabees 10:1-7; see 1 Maccabees 4:36-61). The palm fronds were understood to represent military victory. This suggests that the crowd who welcomed Jesus to Jerusalem expected Jesus to bring them victory, to come as a conquering king. But this king is not at their beck and call. Jesus is not tame.

The people's words to Jesus are another clue about their expectations. When the palm-waving crowd shouted "Hosanna!" or "save please," they echoed Psalm 118:25-26:

[25] Lord, please save us!
   Lord, please let us succeed!

²⁶ The one who enters in the Lord's name is blessed;
we bless all of you from the Lord's house.

These words found in Psalm 118 were "a psalm chanted at major festivals as pilgrims approached the temple," according to Dr. Stanley Saunders, associate professor of New Testament at Columbia Theological Seminary.[8] They expected Jesus to come to them bringing salvation in the name of the Lord, as the son of David. But the one who comes in the name of the Lord comes to purify and cleanse, not just to save. He brings judgment, not validation. Jesus is not safe.

In Matthew 21:12, Jesus enters Jerusalem on a donkey and journeys through the crowds from the city gates directly to the Temple. This is what the people expected. What they didn't expect is what happened when he got there. At the Temple, Jesus encounters people who have come to offer sacrifices, buying, selling, and exchanging currency. In one interpretation, Jesus is angered by the moneychangers and sacrifice sellers taking advantage of hard working folk trying to do right in the eyes of God—many of the people, after all, had traveled a long journey to the Temple, and needed to exchange their foreign currency and purchase animals to sacrifice. They were vulnerable to unfair prices and exchange rates. But in another interpretation, Jesus attacks the very people who have come to worship in the Temple. Jesus quotes Isaiah 56:7 and Jeremiah 7:11 as he turns over the tables, and in Jeremiah 7 the prophet criticizes the unjust people of Judah. They believe that the Temple will be a safe refuge for them, despite their unjust and unfair practices. Therefore, the prophet says that they regard the temple as a den for thieves. In this interpretation, Jesus is similarly calling out the people of Judah and Jerusalem, criticizing them for using Temple worship to mask their lack of justice. It's not just the moneychangers that Jesus casts out, but the religious leaders and worshipers as well.

In the same week that he knocked over tables in the Temple, Jesus would breathe his last breath. Jesus' last week began as he approached the Temple, a place where God's people were supposed to be able to experience the fullness of Yahweh. But the Temple was no longer the Temple that God intended; it was more like a "hideout for crooks." So Jesus turned the tables over.

What would Jesus find if he came to our churches today? What tables would he turn over? Our history is rampant with religious leaders who kill, enslave, and practice genocide on marginalized groups in the name of God. Some clergy use funerals as opportunities for quick altar calls. Some pastors fall into the temptation of preaching a prosperity-based gospel that makes people feel good but provides no depth for the times when life gets challenging. Some ministers preach what some want to hear without listening to what God is actually saying or recognizing where the Holy One is moving. The same danger exists for churchgoers as well as church leaders. How tempting it is to regard God and our religion as a refuge, a safe haven we can retreat into for protection even though our lives create or participate in injustice all around us. Jesus' triumphal entry into Jerusalem and his actions in the Temple remind us that God's coming might rub us the wrong way. God's goodness might judge us and challenge us to a better way of life. Jesus is neither safe nor tame. He is good.

I think part of the challenge of the crowd that greeted Jesus riding into town was that their best intentions were not fully thought through. The crowds were hoping that the Messiah would come to save them on their terms, but Jesus had a greater plan. We often want salvation to happen on our terms, not God's, and our intentions are not fully thought through. Here is one example: Not long ago, Starbucks tried something new with the best of intentions. Baristas were encouraged to write the words *race together* on random cups of coffee. The goal of this project was to initiate conversations regarding race relations.[9] This concept, though intended to "get people talking," didn't provide adequate tools to foster the conversation. Sometimes doing something without listening, pausing, planning, and praying can actually do harm. But the challenge really came when people waiting for a cup of coffee didn't have the adequate tools and ultimately time to talk about such personal matters that have lasted for generations. The initial idea was good; however, the execution failed. Starbucks tried to jump-start something rather than honoring the process that can take time.

It's tempting to hope for a quick, easy solution on our own terms rather than what God has in view. The crowd in Jerusalem cried Hosanna, "save us," without being fully aware of what they were asking God to do. God does come to save, but salvation can be a difficult process. It can start with turning tables over. It involves adopting a new, better way of life that looks more like the kingdom of God that Jesus came to proclaim and embody. It comes through the cross.

So, Jesus rarely fits our expectations; we cannot will him to do what we want. Ultimately, the Messiah was not tame. Jesus was and is good. He is just, merciful, and gracious. He healed the sick and touched those whom society rejected. Jesus ate with outcasts and washed the feet of the lowest of society. He showed us a better way through his life and actions. Looking at the entry into Jerusalem is a good way to take a good long look at what we want Jesus to be and to study who Jesus really was. He is far from tame, and that's a good thing.

Questions for Reflection and Discussion

1. What does the cross mean to you in your life, faith, and everyday actions?
2. What expectations do people around you seem to have of Jesus? How does Jesus overturn some, or all, of these expectations?
3. What faulty expectations do you have about Jesus, and how does the Jesus of Scripture challenge those expectations?

4. What would Jesus find if he came to your church or your home today? What might he overturn in your life?
5. How would this overturning be the beginning of salvation for you or for your faith community?
6. How will you keep the Holy in this week as you consider the intersection between our expectations of Jesus and his life, teachings, death, and resurrection?

Prayer

Jesus, we confess to you that we wave palms one day, but through our actions we are guilty for turning away from you. Forgive us for the times when we settle for quick and easy solutions. There are times when our actions, inactions, and thoughts try to tame you rather than focus on the life you lived. You lived a life full of grace, mercy, and love. Thank you for loving, living, dying, and rising again. There is so much mystery in who you are, what you did, yet we are not a mystery to you. Thank you for who you are and what you are doing; in Jesus' name. Amen.

Focus for the Week

Create a cross with something that you can find in your home. On the cross, write a word or phrase and carry it with you this Holy week. Choose a word or phrase that will help you remain grounded spiritually as we move closer to the cross and grave.

Read the following Scriptures each day. Pause prayerfully before you read. Become aware of your breathing, of the ways you are drawn to this sacred moment, and of the ways you may be distracted. Offer all that is happening to God. Ask for God's guidance as you engage each of the readings.

Monday: Matthew 28:1-5
Tuesday: Matthew 28:6-10
Wednesday: Matthew 28:11-15
Thursday: Matthew 28:16-20
Friday: Matthew 28:1-20
Saturday: Matthew 28:1-10

1. From www.cslewis.org/resource/chronocsl/. Accessed 27 September 2016.

2. From *The Lion, the Witch, and the Wardrobe*, by C. S. Lewis (Collector's edition; Harper Collins, 2000); pages 80 and 182.

3. From www.merriam-webster.com/dictionary/tame. Accessed 27 September 2016.

4. From *The Last Week: What the Gospels Really Teach Us About Jesus's Final Days in Jerusalem*, by Marcus Borg and John Dominic Crossan (HarperOne, 2006); page 3.

5. From T*he Last Week: What the Gospels Really Teach Us About Jesus's Final Days in Jerusalem*, by Marcus Borg and John Dominic Crossan (HarperOne, 2006); page 4.

6. From www.workingpreacher.org/preaching.aspx?commentary_id=2404, by Stanley Saunders. Accessed 27 September 2016.

7. From *Zechariah: A Commentary on His Visions and Prophecies*, by David Baron (Kregel, 2001); page 7.

8. From www.workingpreacher.org/preaching.aspx?commentary_id=2404, by Stanley Saunders. Accessed 27 September 2016.

9. From www.rollingstone.com/culture/news/starbucks-scraps-their-race-together-initiative-20150322. Accessed 27 September 2016.

If a Tree Falls in the Woods...

Scripture: Read Matthew 28:1-20

"Don't be afraid. I know that you are looking for Jesus who was crucified. He isn't here, because he's been raised from the dead, just as he said." (Matthew 28:5-6)

If a tree falls in the woods, would it make a sound? OK, that's not really how the question is worded. It's really, "If a tree falls in a forest and no one is around to hear it, does it make a sound?" This question is so popular, it has its own Wikipedia page.[1] So what do you think? If a tree falls in the woods but nobody is around to hear it, does it make a sound?

What if a man sits in a tree and draws national attention? While I was finishing this book, a man sat atop an eighty-foot-tall sequoia tree outside of a major downtown Seattle department store for more than twenty-four hours. This tree is affectionately referred to by local Seattleites as the Seattle Christmas tree. For a couple of days during Holy Week, a man sat perched near the top of this historic tree and drew the attention of the nation. When he finally came down, folks had a mixture of responses. Many were saddened by the damage done to the historic tree; others worried about the amount of tax dollars invested in the police, fire fighters, and others who enticed him to come down from the tree.

Still others cried out for justice and asked that he face the consequences of his actions. One person said, "It caused a lot of inconvenience, it cost a lot of money, and he damaged a tree nurtured since the '70s – Seattle's Christmas tree. That's the real crime," he said.[2] No one seemed to be concerned about his well-being.

Personally, I'm saddened whenever nature is hurt or damaged in any way. That said, I'm not sure damage to the tree is the crime here. A man slept in the branches of a great Christmas tree during Holy Week, and society neglected the simple fact that he was a human being with a name and a story. Did we forget? Or did we not care? From everything I heard in response to the story, it seemed that people cared more about the tree than the man. But in the life, ministry, death, and resurrection of Jesus, Christians are challenged to reexamine our priorities and shape them toward justice, first and foremost for vulnerable humans in our midst.

Over the course of this book, we have taken time to study some of the prophets in the Hebrew Scriptures who gave us glimpses of the Messiah in Jesus Christ. Time and time again, the prophets' message to the people of God was to anticipate and expect that the Messiah will come. The Kingdom is coming, they said through their calls for justice. This was the wind in the wilderness.

In the first chapter, we unpacked Isaiah's message to God's people about the Kingdom to come. I shared the story of a friend who likened her work to building a skyscraper. In order to build a skyscraper, years of preparation are required before an inch is built upward, and it all begins by digging a hole. Through this Lenten season, we have taken time to consider what kind of a hole we are in. This hole isn't the finished product. And this world isn't the final product either. We looked at words that can harm and work for good, every bit as powerful as sticks and stones, through the prophet Jeremiah. We took a deeper look at the life of Hosea and his family as we sought to understand Yahweh. We even went for a run with Jonah! Along the way, we paused with Job as we focused on becoming present as we wait. In the last chapter, we looked at Jesus' entry into Jerusalem, using the words of the prophet Zechariah to gain deeper insight.

As we made our approach toward Easter, we waved our palm branches, examining our own hopes, expectations, and desires. Along the way to Easter Sunday, significant events happened in the final week of Jesus' life. We remember, for instance, the Passover Meal that led to Communion as we celebrate it today. We reflect on Jesus, fully human and fully divine, assuming the role of a servant and washing his disciples' feet. We remember the cross and the horror of the crucifixion of Jesus. And today, we celebrate that Jesus has risen! This is the very thing toward which the wind in the wilderness has been pointing all along: the vindication of the one who came to serve, the victory of peace over violence and life over death.

It's imperative that we keep this good news before us, holding it in our minds, as we walk through life after Easter Sunday. It's so easy to forget that we worship the one who has been raised from the dead, and that this renews our own commitment to the justice that the prophets proclaimed. When I was in high school, I preached a sermon at my private Christian school about the need to be matchsticks for Jesus. I stood in the middle of a small crowd of students and talked about how the Holy Spirit would be our gasoline and we needed to be on fire for Jesus. I had good intentions in my metaphor about matchsticks and gasoline, but didn't have the greatest result. Not everyone can be on spiritual fire for God one hundred percent of the time. There might be a scant few out there, but that's a pretty difficult state to maintain. We mere mortals need regular reminders of Christ's victory at Easter to renew our own spirits and rekindle our own commitment to Kingdom living.

I recently reconnected with an old friend. I had the privilege to serve as his youth minister for most of his adolescent life. During the time I knew him, he struggled with alcohol and drug addiction. He stepped away from church, not feeling like he was safe or accepted in church. He said, "It's really hard to feel like the Christian God and his house of worship is a safe place for us, unless we are also surrounded by a bunch of other people who are just as sick as we are, trying to navigate this thing we call life." I'm grateful that this man was so willing to share his story. His words were so profound. They continue to resonate with where I am in my faith life. What a poignant reminder of our calling as a people of faith to be honest about life's struggles. The good news of Easter is meant to speak directly to all of us, who are "just as sick" as everyone else." Our calling isn't to hold other people to some impossible vision of justice. It is to celebrate the justice that Christ ushered in, expressing it in our lives and in our relationships. We are Easter people, who have felt not just the wind in the wilderness, but the fullness of the Holy Spirit moving in our midst!

The Resurrection Story

Now let's ask our question a different way: If a tree falls in the woods and there were people to hear it, but they deny it, does it make a sound? Let's take a closer look at Matthew 28:11-15.

> Now as the women were on their way, some of the guards came into the city and told the chief priests everything that had happened. They met with the elders and decided to give a large sum of money to the soldiers. They told them, "Say that Jesus' disciples came at night and stole his body while you were sleeping. And if the governor hears about this, we will take care of it with him so you will have nothing to worry about." So the soldiers took the money and did as they were told. And this report has spread throughout all Judea to this very day.

In the Gospel of Matthew, the people in charge convinced the soldiers to lie about what they had experienced. The people in charge denied that it happened. But the Gospel of Matthew makes clear that there is no denying the Resurrection. There were witnesses—two women who came to the tomb—and there was even an earthquake and a message from Jesus himself:

> After the Sabbath, at dawn on the first day of the week, Mary Magdalene and the other Mary came to look at the tomb. Look, there was a great earthquake, for an angel from the Lord came down from heaven. Coming to the stone, he rolled it away and sat on it. Now his face was like lightning and his clothes as white as snow. The guards were so terrified of him that they shook with fear and became like dead men. But the angel said to the women, "Don't be afraid. I know that you are looking for Jesus who was crucified. He isn't here, because he's been raised from the dead, just as he said. Come, see the place where they laid him. Now hurry, go and tell his disciples, 'He's been raised from the dead. He's going on ahead of you to Galilee. You will see him there.' I've given the message to you."
>
> With great feat and excitement, they hurried away from the tomb and ran to tell his disciples. But Jesus met them and greeted them. They came and grabbed his feet and worshipped him. Then Jesus said to them, "Don't be afraid. Go and tell my brothers that I am going into Galilee. They will see me there."
>
> (Matthew 28:1-10)

The resurrection of Jesus is a reality that we cannot deny. From the angelic proclamation of Jesus' birth through the angelic proclamation of his resurrection, Matthew's Gospel consistently highlights the fulfillment of the Hebrew prophets' message that the Messiah would come. And two women were the first to witness it, the first to receive the good news that Jesus is risen.

At first light, these two women brought spices to the tomb to prepare Jesus' body according to their custom. Matthew paints a picture of two women named Mary who wanted to be near their loved one. They got up early, before anyone else, to be near him.

There's a cemetery not very far from where I serve at Bothell United Methodist Church. I've had the honor of presiding over many funerals there, including the funerals of my grandparents. When I first started my marathon training, I often ran to the cemetery to run laps around it. I liked running a local trail called the Burke-Gilman trail for long runs, but for shorter runs I found the cemetery both therapeutic and peaceful. I would often stop by my grandparents' graves. There was something very peaceful about visiting their graveside in the early morning when no one else was around. Maybe that's why the two Marys went to visit Jesus' graveside. I wonder if they wanted to go at a time when no one else would be around, to gain some quiet, lonely time with the one whom they had loved.

Tell the Good News

But the graveside scene from Matthew's perspective is the last thing from peaceful. Matthew describes an earthquake, a bright shining angel descending, guards becoming "like dead men," and Jesus giving the two women a message that would change the world. Matthew has a flare for the dramatic. But what's really significant is, both the angel and Jesus instruct the women to tell someone else about what they have seen. The Christian message is good news that we are called, even commanded, to tell others about! It is our privilege to tell others about this dramatic, world-changing event, witnessing to the way that we have experienced the risen Christ.

Of course, there are effective ways to tell others about Christ, and not-so-effective ways to do it. The other day I was at Starbucks and three people got into a heated discussion about religion. Persons A and B were trying to convince person C that he needed Jesus. Here is how the conversation went:

Person A: You need Jesus, because he is like an eraser for all of your sins.

Person C: Do you mean Zombie Jesus? You know, he rose from the dead. So he's a zombie right?

Person A: You need to get your ticket to the next spot (heaven).

Person C: What about this spot?

Person A: Earth, too late.

While Persons A and C talked over one another; Person B sat quietly and attentively.

Person A got up to answer the phone and walked away.

Person B: May I ask your name?

Person C: Thank you for asking . . .

Persons B and C proceeded to have a deep discussion about their lives. Person C shared his story and asked to hear Person B's story. Some time later, Person A returned and immediately interrupted the conversation saying, "You just need to repeat these words: 'Jesus Christ are you real?' I promise you that he will respond, and your life will be better!

Person C: [seriously repeats] Jesus Christ are you real? [Long pause] I don't feel anything.

With that, Person A got up and said to Person C, "At least I tried."

Rob Bell once said in his book *Velvet Elvis* that if the gospel isn't good news for everybody, then it isn't good news for anybody. Today, we celebrate that the gospel is good news for everybody. But it's our responsibility to communicate that good news in a way that honors other people's questions, struggles, and thoughts, so that they can really, truly understand just how good the news is!

If a tree falls in the woods and no one is around to witness it, it still falls. The gospel message that Jesus lived, died, and rose again is true. Maybe the question for us is how we live this truth in such a way that other people can see its realness in our lives. The time of talking over one another is done. I'm not sure it's ever had a place in the first place. It's time for us to stop waiting for our turn to speak and take the time to learn from one another. It's time for us to bear witness to the truth of Jesus' resurrection, the victory of life over death, by the way that we embody justice in the way that we live. It's time to proclaim that Jesus is risen through our actions, our relationships, and our outlook of love.

Here is how I choose to witness to the resurrection: by pointing to the beauty in each and every person. This is, I think, at the root of the justice that the prophets proclaimed and that Jesus embodied and fulfilled. Every person is beautiful, every person is valuable, and our communities and individual actions must honor that beauty.

When is the last time you saw something really beautiful? Maybe it's a special person in your life. Maybe it's a child or a pet. Maybe it's when you watched a sunrise or sunset and you knew that you were in the presence of something truly beautiful and sacred. Everything I read about in Scripture tells me that Jesus sees something beautiful in each of us.

I asked my congregation and social media, "How do you respond when people tell you that you are beautiful?" Here is a sample of the responses:

- I get very uncomfortable, but maybe even more annoyed because I don't think it's particularly true so I don't know what to say. But also I think looks are usually the least interesting thing about a person.
- I just told my wife she is beautiful. Her response, "HA! DJ put you up to that!" **SIGH** Thanks, Pastor . . .
- Any flattery I may feel is fleeting. But it is different if the words come from someone who truly knows me—who has seen me in varying stages of "undone-ness," both

in outward appearance and emotions. I can sense that they see and respond to me as a whole person. When someone I love says, "You are beautiful," I can accept it. I feel honored.

- I want to believe that they're telling the truth. But I don't because I don't feel beautiful.
- It took me a long time to claim my beauty. I also grew up in a family that never said you were beautiful. I'm thankful for the husband who named that for me. And I do think we need a broader definition of beautiful—even physical beauty comes in a dazzling array of variations.

We worship God who knows us, who sees each one of us and says I love you; you are beautiful; you are forgiven; the world is a better place because of you.

Jesus always loved you
    He always loved you
        He always will love you
            Jesus knows the way out of the grave
                He knows the way. He is the way.

Today, let us sit in the mystery of faith. If the Pope washed and kissed the feet of Muslim, Christian, and Hindu refugees at a center for asylum-seekers just outside Rome, then maybe we should take his cue and celebrate the good news that is for everyone.[3] Jesus lived, died, and rose again, purely for the love of you and me.

We worship a God who knows our name. Let us be the church we are called be, allowing space for all people to experience sacred moments and say to one another, "You are forgiven, and you are beautiful." We worship Jesus, who appreciates our great joys, our deep hurts, and everything in between. We worship Jesus, who understands our loneliness and our fear of being abandoned.

May you experience Jesus in a new and profound way.

May you find Jesus in the simplest and humblest moments of your life, as you strive to live that life characterized by justice.

Whether you need proof for your head or your heart, may you find it today.

May you be for the world wind in the wilderness. Amen.

Questions for Reflection and Discussion

1. Do you believe that you are beautiful?
2. How will you take one more step this week toward living a life that is beautiful?
3. What does it mean to you that Jesus loves you and knows your name?
4. How will you honor the beauty and sacredness of each person you encounter this week?
5. How will you tell someone else about the good news of Jesus' resurrection?

Prayer

Sacred One, a tree has fallen in the woods. The tomb stone has been rolled away. You have lived the lives we live and defeated death. You alone know the way out of the wilderness, just as you know the way out of the tomb. Thank you for knowing my name. Thank you for loving creation and all that is within her. May your will be done. May your love be shared. May it begin with me so that all of creation will sing your praises. In your son's name, Jesus the Christ, I pray. Amen.

Focus for the Week

Write your name on a sticky note. Keep it in a place that you will see several times a day (bathroom mirror, car, and so forth). Each time you see it, take three deep breaths and contemplate the amazing significance that Jesus loves you and knows your name.

Read the following Scriptures each day. Pause prayerfully before you read. Become aware of your breathing, of the ways you are drawn to this sacred moment, and of the ways you may be distracted. Offer all that is happening to God. Ask for God's guidance as you engage each of the readings.

Monday: John 21:1-2
Tuesday: John 21: 3
Wednesday: John 21: 4-6
Thursday: John 21: 7-8
Friday: John 21: 9-14
Saturday: John 21:1-14

1. From *en.wikipedia.org/wiki/If_a_tree_falls_in_a_forest*. Accessed 27 September 2016.

2. From *www.seattletimes.com/seattle-news/man-spends-night-in-80-foot-tree-in-downtown-seattle-builds-makeshift-nest/*. Accessed 27 September 2016.

3. From *www.npr.org/sections/thetwo-way/2016/03/25/471847938/pope-francis-follows-easter-traditions-while-changing-some-of-them*. Accessed 27 September 2016.